MINOLTA 9000

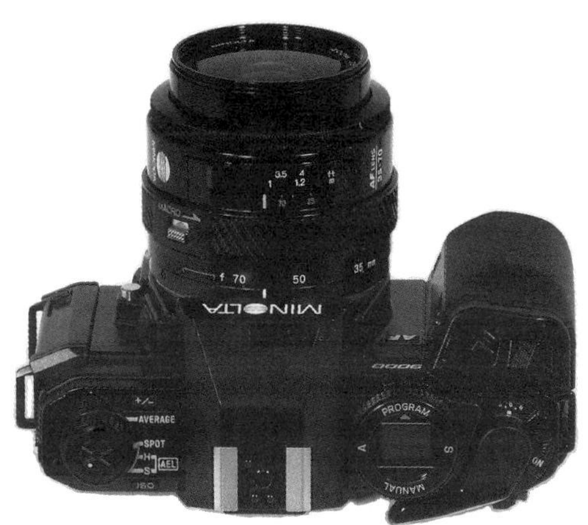

Andrew Mannheim

HOVE~FOUNTAIN BOOKS

In U.S.A. and Canada

the Minolta 9000 is known as the

MAXXUM 9000

All text, illustrations and data apply to cameras with either name
U.S. Edition ISBN 0-86343-084-8

MINOLTA 9000

First English Edition June 1987
English Translation from the original German
by Liselotte Sperl
Edited by George Wakefield
Series Editor Dennis Laney
Typeset by Direct Image Photosetting, Hove
Printed in Great Britain by
Purnell Book Production Ltd

ISBN 0-86343-069-4

Published by
HOVE FOUNTAIN BOOKS

<table>
<tr><td>45 The Broadway
Tolworth
Surrey KT6 7DW</td><td>34 Church Road
Hove
Sussex BN3 2GJ</td></tr>
<tr><td>U.K. Trade Distribution by
Fountain Press Ltd
address
as above</td><td>U.S.A. Distributor
Seven Hills Books
49 Central Avenue, Suite 300
Cincinnati, Ohio 45202</td></tr>
</table>

Contents

The automatic setting functions of the Minolta 9000 leave the photographer free to concentrate on picture creation. The emphasis on the foreground was achieved by the use of a wide-angle lens.
Photo: Hermine Gsteu

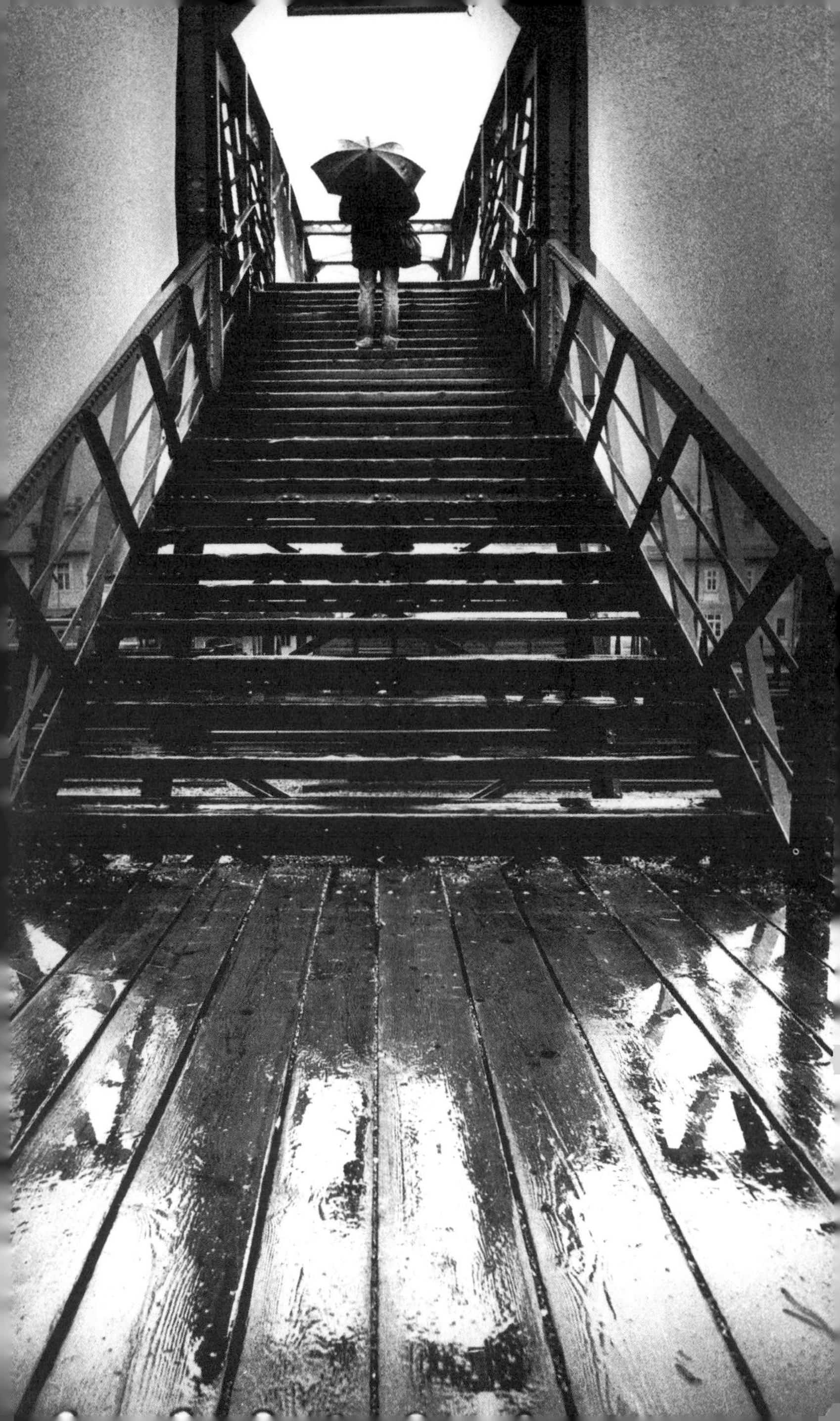

A Unique System

Camera systems tend to develop consistently: Successive models remain compatible with existing lenses and accessories. The idea is to keep the camera user faithful to the brand and to encourage him to update his outfit with new versions whenever they appear.

Yet leading SLR camera maker Minolta abandoned this almost sacred marketing principle early in 1985. With the model 7000, the firm launched a novel camera line with full-system autofocusing. For after much heart-searching Minolta had decided that autofocus would be too difficult to realise efficiently with their previous system.

Sharpness by Motor

Primitive automatic exposure (AE) control existed in cameras some 50 years ago but it has become very sophisticated in modern Minolta models. Automatic focusing on the other hand appeared on the market only about 10 years ago, mainly in compact 35mm cameras where an electronic distance-measuring system controls a motor to focus a permanently built-in lens.

Such motorised focusing is rather more difficult to realise in a single-lens reflex (SLR) with a range of interchangeable lenses differing widely in design and focusing mechanism. Some camera makers tried it by installing a focusing motor in the lens, controlled by an electronic sharpness, rather than distance-measuring system in the camera. That made such autofocus of AF lenses bulky and not very versatile but the camera was able to use existing lenses without autofocus. The ideal engineering solution is to have the focusing motor in the camera plus a matched extensive lens range with a specially smooth focusing mechanism.

That has been Minolta's way. However, it involved deliberately creating a new equipment system based exclusively on AF lenses. Self-contained and comprehensive, this has proved singularly successful. Today it already includes three camera models; the versatile Minolta 7000, a trimmed-down and lower-priced model 5000 and, as a top model for the professional and advanced amateur, the Minolta 9000 – the subject of this book.

The Professional Minolta 9000

How do a professional's camera expectations differ from

The large handgrip is a noticeable feature of the Minolta 9000. The batteries feeding the various functions are stored in the grip. The camera is shown with the standard lens.

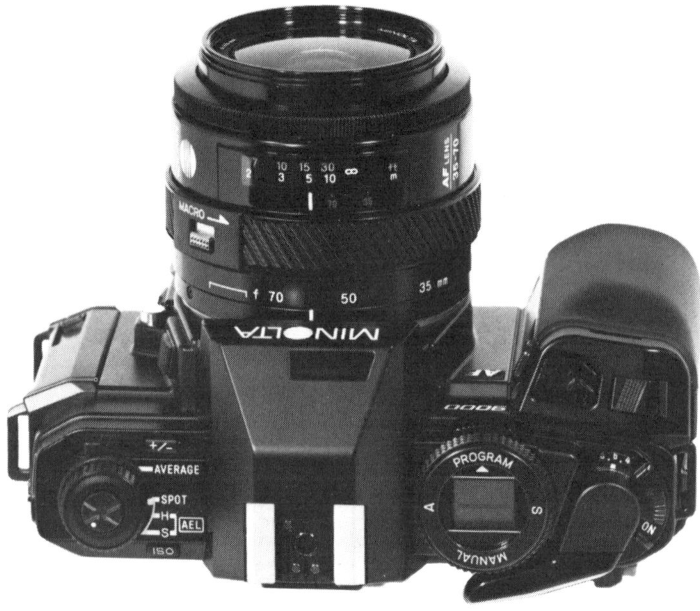

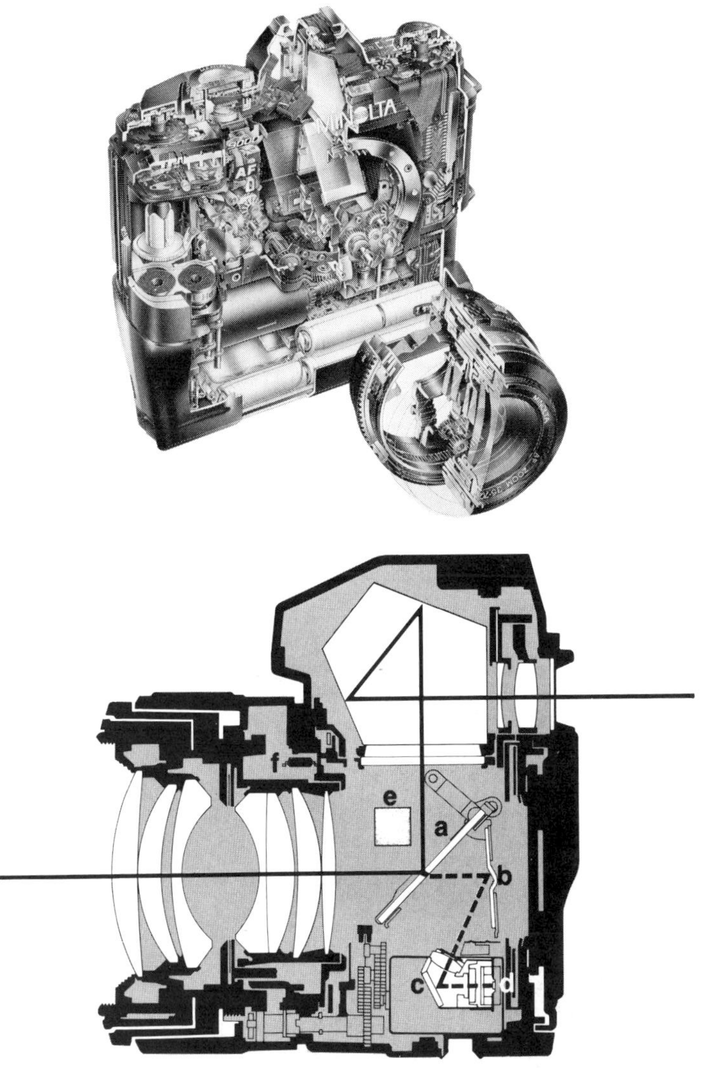

In the Minolta 9000 the image projected by the lens is directed by the main mirror (a) to the prism viewfinder (top) as is usual in SLR cameras. The main mirror allows part of the light to fall on the auxiliary mirror (b). From there part of the light is directed via a further mirror (c) and its own lens arrangement to the CCD-sensor (d) of the focusing metering system. The light from the rest of the auxiliary mirror is directed to the light metering system (metering cell, right).

those of an amateur? What indeed distinguishes the professional from the amateur? For the professional earning his living, the camera is a tool. For the amateur it may sometimes be almost a toy. This is not an exclusive distinction; many features giving professional versatility are also fascinating to play with.

The serious camera user, both professional and amateur, looks for an instrument that best meets the widest range of his picture-taking needs. He looks firstly for versatility, secondly for convenience and thirdly for reliability. The snapshooter may have similar expectations, though usually with different priorities.

The camera system with interchangeable lenses and accessories provides the versatility; exposure and focusing automation offer the convenience. For the professional reliability becomes vital. That's why professionals take some time to accept technical innovations. But the evolution of, for instance, exposure automation has shown that sooner or later handling convenience scores even over this distrust. Here are the principal features of the Minolta 9000:

○ First, it offers highly sophisticated exposure measurement and control. Metering modes cover both centre-weighted full-area readings and spot readings. With the latter you can selectively measure mid-tones, highlights or shadows. Automatic exposure control modes comprise aperture-priority, shutter speed-priority, programmed automation with optional aperture or shutter speed override and of course manual control. The idea of this range of modes is to provide, as automatically as possible, correctly exposed shots more or less every time.

○ Secondly, as mentioned, it has autofocus. This system not only focuses the lens sharply on any object centred in the finder; it also adjusts focus as the distance changes. With the motor drive you can

14

even interlock the release so as to expose the picture only when it is sharply focused.

○ Thirdly, its accessories provide a really extensive system. This covers not only an impressive lens range but also flash units with further automation features; a motor drive with a choice of framing rates, rapid motorised rewinding and presettable picture sequences, plus data- and program-backs with various remote control and interval timing features.

○ Finally, the whole camera is designed for heavy-duty use. The body is a light-alloy die casting and not, as in many current amateur models, Minolta's included, a compound metal/plastic hybrid. The all-metal shutter with hardened aluminium alloy blades and titanium control levers yields a fastest $1/4000$ second shutter speed and synchronises electronic flash up to $1/250$ second. The lens mounting flange on the camera is stainless steel.

Technical Overkill

This summary specification looks impressive and at first sight daunting, for the various operating modes involve controls, displays and information that you have to act on. How on earth can one learn all this?

With many automatic cameras, sophisticated technology takes over for the user. With such point-and-shoot models you literally point the camera and press the button. That needs no book reading. But to utilise the full scope of modern technology, you do have to find out more about it; that goes for cameras as much as for home computers, or for hi-fi systems. The Minolta 9000 is not a point-and-shoot camera, though you can use it even in that fully automatic mode. The aim of this book is to familiarise you with its more extended scope and its applications.

Controls and Functions

As is usual with single lens reflex cameras, the Minolta 9000 shows a correct image in the viewfinder with respect to framing and sharpness of the future photograph. This is the image produced by the lens and projected into the viewfinder by a mirror, and which will subsequently be projected onto the film when the mirror is folded away. The mirror system also directs the light to a metering cell and a focusing sensor.

These functions are accomplished by an unusually-shaped auxiliary mirror behind the partially transparent main mirror. The sharpness sensor is provided by the offset centre section, whilst the remaining mirror surface supplies the light meter cell. The centre section is clearly seen when the lens is removed, but it cannot be distinguished through the viewfinder as the latter receives light from the whole of the surface of the main mirror. The only feature in the viewfinder is a small rectangle in the middle of a central circle. These are the metering areas for focusing and spot exposure metering respectively. Below the viewfinder screen are various displays, which I shall describe in detail later on. Meanwhile here are the operating controls:

View from the Top

First we shall examine the camera body, starting with a view from the top. With the lens pointing forward, i.e. in the shooting direction, you hold the left side of the camera in your left hand and the right side with the right hand. Any further references to "left" and "right" in this book should be understood in this way.

First the top plate. The knob at the left-hand side when pulled out turns into the rewind crank. Used together with the black slide key (back panel lock) in front of it, the back panel is opened. Fully depressed, this knob becomes the metering type selector, allowing various settings: AVERAGE, SPOT, etc. Above these inscriptions, next to the back panel lock, is the exposure correction key marked +/-. Beneath the inscriptions is a key bearing the legend ISO for the setting and checking of film speed.

In the centre, on top of the prism housing, is the accessory shoe with flash contacts. The large contact fires the flashgun synchronous with the shutter sequence, the others convey various signals between camera and flashgun, amongst these being the automatic control of flash duration. The window on the sloping prism roof serves to illuminate the viewfinder display.

On the right of the prism housing is the exposure-mode, or function selector. This is a large knurled knob whose four positions marked MANUAL, A, PROGRAM and S engage at the triangular stop position. In the centre of this knob is the display area. Shutter speed and

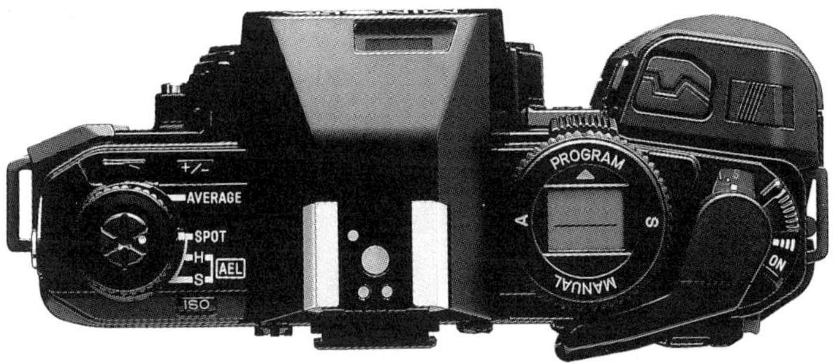

Most operating elements are situated on top of the camera. The knob on the left is the metering type selector and serves also as the rewind crank and, in connection with the key in front of it, to release the lock of the back panel. The two smaller keys next to it are for exposure correction and display and setting of film speed. In the centre of the viewfinder housing is the accessory shoe. To the right of that is the shooting mode selector and within it, the liquid crystal display. Further to the right is the film advance lever, and in front of that the frame counter, the main switch and, on top of the protruding hand grip the release and the slide switch for the self-timer.

aperture, or film speed, is displayed here by an LCD (Liquid Crystal Display). These displays, complementary to the information shown in the viewfinder display, appear on lightly depressing the release button, the ISO key or the exposure correction key (+/-) and always remain visible for about 10 seconds.

The various displays in the data field, and the complementary displays in the viewfinder, are explained in detail in the chapters dealing with their particular uses. Furthermore, the chapter 'Data Display' gives a comprehensive list of all the possible display combinations.

The transport lever to the right of the function selector transports the film by one frame after each exposure, and simultaneously cocks the shutter. In its initial position the lever is inclined about 30° to the back panel, but it can be folded flush to the back panel. The lever describes a 130° path to transport one frame, which may be performed by a single or several partial movements.

Immediately in front of the lever is the frame counter, displaying the current frame number. The main switch to the right of the transport lever shows alternatively ON or OFF (ON may optionally be accompanied by a bleep tone). If the camera is switched off, the horizontal bar, the shutter speed indication, and the aperture value in the LCD frame all disappear. Otherwise the bar is always visible when the camera is switched on, even if the shutter speed and the aperture value are not shown.

The body projection in front of the wind-on lever serves as a handgrip and battery compartment. On top of this compartment is the irregularly shaped, five-sided release button, and next to it a small slide key for the self-timer. The release button is a touch-sensitive key. This means that certain functions are activated simply by touching it with the finger, without pressure. Lastly, there is the stopping-down lever on the left of the handgrip, which is moved out to check depth of field.

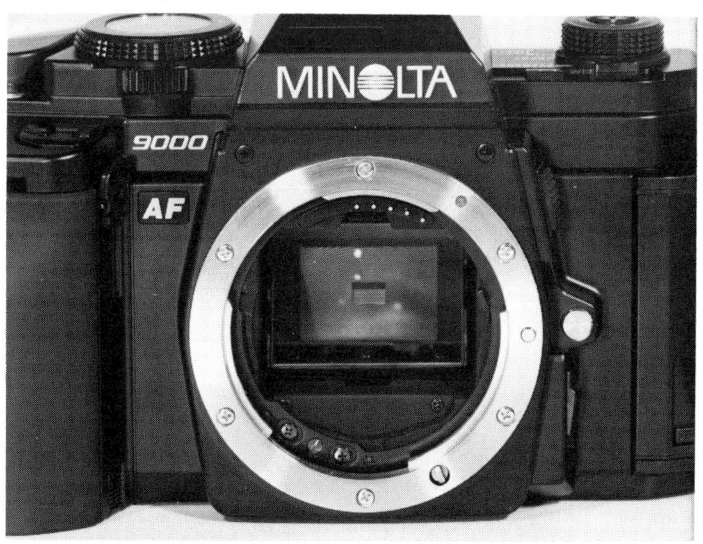

The important elements in this front view are the shutter speed switch (between "9000" and shooting mode selector), above that at the inside of the handgrip is the stop-down lever and the LED display for self-timer (barely visible from this position). To the left of the lens flange, half way up, is the bayonet release button, and above that the AF switch and below that the aperture switch.

From the Front

Let's start from the right, the handgrip side, where we just finished examining the camera from the top. Towards the top edge is the rectangular LED signal window of the self-timer, and to its left the slide timer switch which is used to set the shutter speeds in manual operation, or the shutter speed/aperture value combination in automatic operation.

The remaining operational controls at the front of the camera are on the other side. Depressing the chromed round button releases the lock for the lens bayonet. The slide switch beneath selects manual (M) or automatic

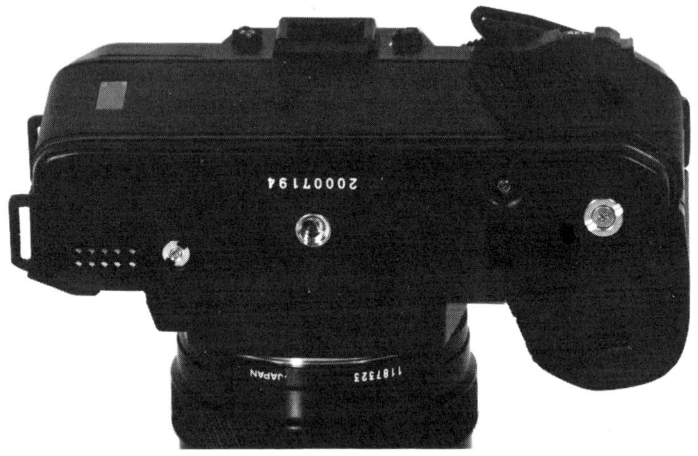

The camera base accommodates motor contacts for film rewind (left), transport coupling (right) and rewind release and the tripod thread. The battery compartment lever is visible at the bottom of the handgrip.

focusing (AF). The second, unmarked black slide switch (aperture switch), is used to reset the aperture value in manual operation, or the shutter speed/aperture value combination in the other shooting modes.

At the bottom left is the remote control connection, covered by a slide cover.

From the Bottom and the Back

At the left-hand side of the camera base is the motor drive connection, ten gold contacts, and next to these the rewind coupling. In the centre of the base is the tripod thread, which is also used to secure the motor drive to the body. Further to the right is the rewind release and the cam for the transport coupling.

In addition there are three guide holes in the camera base, one on each side of the contact strip to the left, and the third at the far right edge. These guides ensure proper contact of the motor drive. When buying a new

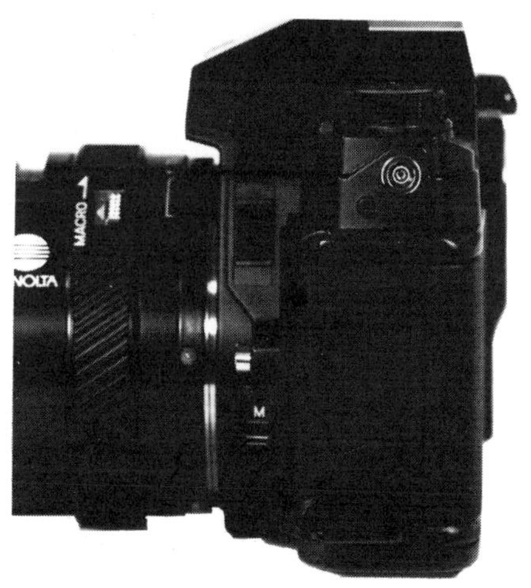

Details on the left side of the camera: top right, the second synchronization contact, beneath that the remote control connection. On the outside of the prism housing '(from bottom to top) are the AF switch (in position M in this view), the release button for lens bayonet and the black aperture setting switch.

camera the base is protected by a clear plastic foil to prevent scratching. This in no way interferes with any of the camera's functions and may be left on, even when attaching the motor drive, as long as it looks presentable.

The grip on the right is a rather prominent feature of the back panel. Together with the handgrip it affords secure and steady support of the camera.

The film speed and number of frames, printed on most modern makes of film, can be read through the film window on the left-hand side of the back panel, but the film inside is protected against incident light.

Above the rear panel, at the back of the camera's pentaprism housing, is the viewfinder eyepiece. To its left is an eyepiece dioptre correction adjustment, and to its right the eyepiece cover, which is necessary in some applications to avoid unwanted light entering through the viewfinder and thus producing incorrect metering results. At the right there are two keys, the one marked AEL is the exposure memory button and the unmarked one, which may be pushed to the left, is the multiple exposure key. On the left-hand narrow panel is a synchronization contact for flash photography. Both side panels have lugs for carrying straps, two on the left and one on the right for adjustable positions.

Lenses and Lens Changing

The lenses themselves have hardly any operating controls, at least not the f/1.4,50mm or the f/1.7,50mm standard lenses. They both possess only a knurled front ring. Turning this ring moves the lens out of the front bezel. At the same time a scale is displayed through a

The distance scale on the lens is given in metres and feet. The depth of field scale beneath shows that, for example, with a setting at infinity and aperture f/22, the depth of field will extend from 3m to infinity.

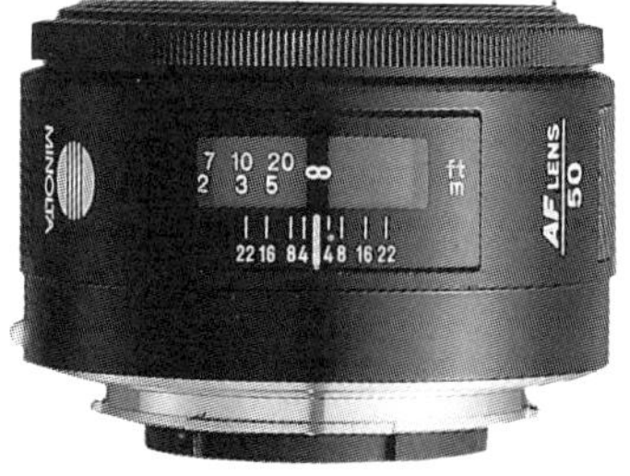

Holding the lens in the left hand as shown, the left thumb depresses the release button and the hand turns the lens anti clockwise, and removes it.

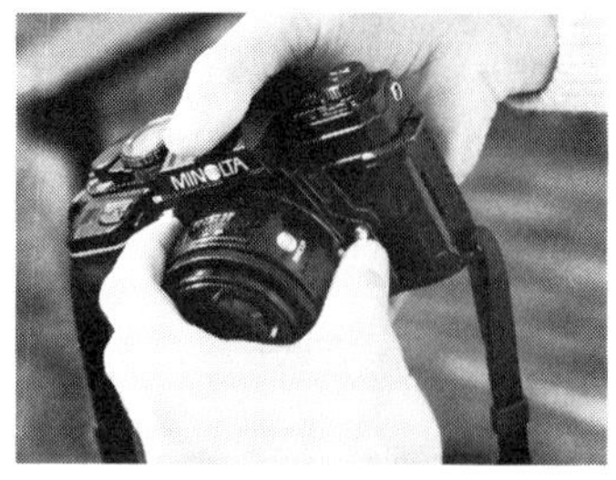

This is how another lens is fitted: left thumb on right marker, inserting the lens under the prism projection into the bayonet.

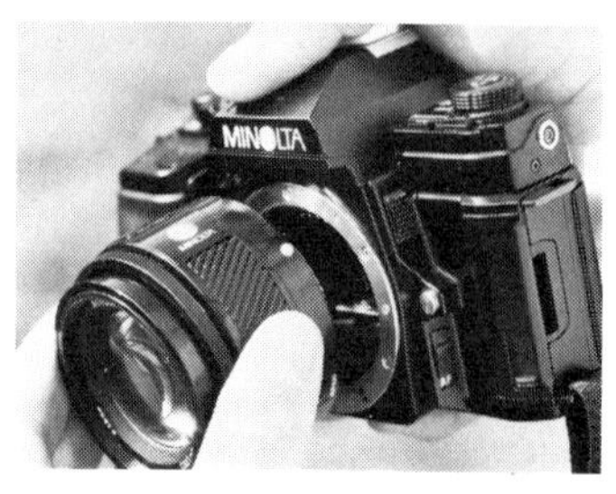

window at the top. This is the distance scale in metres (m, white) and feet (f, yellow): the value actually set is the figure against the thick white index line. At each side of the index line are lines to indicate depth of field.

The front ring may be turned quite easily when the AF switch on the camera is in the 'M' position. On selecting the 'AF' position the movement of the front ring becomes heavy. This is due to the fact that the setting ring on the lens is coupled with the motor inside the camera when AF has been selected.

Let's get onto a more intimate footing with our Minolta 9000 by removing the lens. This is done by depressing the chromed bayonet release button next to the red bead on the lens. The whole lens is then turned about a sixth of a turn to the left and may then be removed from the camera.

To re-insert the lens, hold it so that the red bead is aligned with the red dot on the lens flange, push it into the bayonet ring and turn it to the right until it engages. You have mastered the first operation on your camera.

The easiest way to change a lens is to hold the camera in the right hand and the lens in the left so that the left thumb presses on the release button. The left hand can then turn and remove the lens. This is possible even with larger lenses. It is almost as easy when you are carrying the camera on a strap round your neck; it is even possible to perform this operation with one hand only.

The red bead is a good touch guide: you can find it with your left thumb without looking. In its correct location it is supposed to be level with the lens release button, which is also easily discernible by touch only. With a little practice you can change your lenses blindfold.

Before moving on, here is one good bit of advice on lens changing. Always put the front and rear caps on every lens that is not attached to the camera. The caps

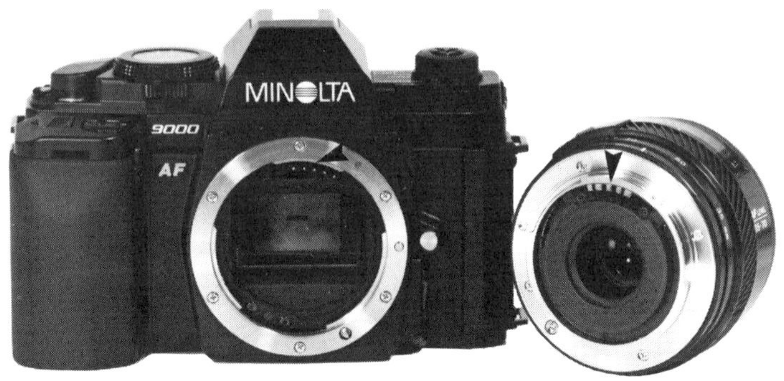

Two special characteristics of the Minolta lens flange are the electrical. contacts for the transfer of aperture scale and other information between camera and lens (arrows), and the coupling spindle for the focusing drive.

protect the delicate surfaces against dust, fingermarks and scratches. This is an important habit that is easily adopted and much less trouble than having to constantly clean the lens. The same precaution also applies to the camera when no lens is fitted.

Coupling Elements and Contacts

The absence of any aperture-setting control on the lens is unusual. This function is taken over by an electrical device within the camera. Five gold contacts provided for this purpose are on the rear lens bezel; the five pins inside the bayonet ring on the camera provide the contact. The latter provide information to the camera's electronics, via a memory chip (ROM - Read Only Memory) integrated in the lens, about the largest and smallest possible aperture values, focal length and other data. These data provide the basis for the selection and control functions of the automatic exposure mode.

The available aperture range is inscribed on the lens. The largest aperture or lens speed is given in the form 1:1.4, say, the smallest in brackets (22) after it. For some zoom lenses there is a second aperture value stated after the bracket, i.e. for the 28-85mm zoom the legend would be 1:3.5(22)-4.5. In this case the lens speed varies with focal length: from f/3.5 at 28mm to f/4.5 at 85mm. Only stopping down to the working aperture is performed mechanically, namely by an electrically controlled coupling ring within the camera and the diaphragm lever on the lens. Activating the diaphragm lever will close the aperture towards the smallest value.

The other important coupling element in the lens is the drive shaft of its focusing movement. The focusing motor in the camera automatically sets the correct focusing distance via a clutch protruding through the camera bayonet flange and engaging with the lens-focusing drive shaft. The clutch is engaged when the AF-switch is set to AF and disengaged when it is set to M for manual focusing. The movement of the shaft in the lens can be observed by moving the knurled lens ring with the lens detached from the camera.

These coupling elements, contacts and drive shaft, are new to the AF lenses of the Minolta 9000 and the Minolta 7000. That is the reason why Minolta were forced to introduce an entirely new lens series and new rear lens bezels for these autofocus cameras.

The Viewfinder

Before we actually try out the camera, let us take a look through the viewfinder. In modern SLR cameras the viewfinder serves on the one hand to view the image that will later be produced as the photograph, and on the other, particularly with the present-day models, as a command centre for exposure settings. Photographers all over the world debate whether the range of signals and information provided are really desirable or not. One is certain though that the versatility of a sophisticated SLR camera depends on the provision of this information.

Viewfinder Displays:
1 Focusing screen, **2** Exposure metering circle with 5.5mm diameter, **3** AF target field 1.25x2.5mm, **4** LED for focusing check, **5** LED for flash-ready display. **In the LCD field: 6** Shutter speed or film speed value, **7** Automatic Function, **8** Aperture Value, **9** Manual Function, **10** Exposure correction or exposure error in manual operation, **11** Symbol for type of metering.

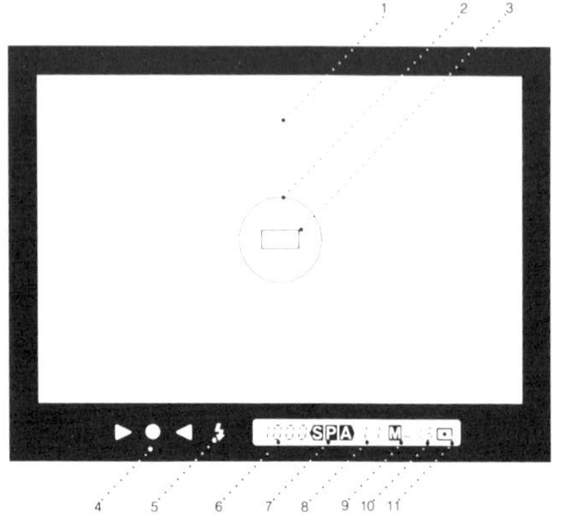

Viewing the image is facilitated by the apparently near life-size image on the focusing screen which shows the exact framing and focus, as is usual with SLR cameras. To be exact, the viewfinder image is only 94% of the size of the actual frame. This cropping of the frame corresponds exactly to the area that would be cropped by a slide mount. The viewfinder therefore shows exactly what would be shown in the final slide. For prints also this is usually no problem because most labs trim the negative as a matter of course. However, it is important that the section of frame shown corresponds to the focal length of the lens employed, particularly for all zoom settings, and that the reduced field of view for close-ups is automatically taken into account. As for the degree of sharpness visible in the viewfinder, and for checking the depth of field by the stop-down key, it is just as important that the sharpness is accurately shown for all lenses and distance settings.

A small rectangle measuring 1.25x2.5mm within a circular outline of 5.5mm diameter in the centre of the viewfinder appears on the otherwise quite normal focusing screen. The rectangle is the target field for focusing, and the circle is the metering field for selective exposure metering. For spot metering please refer to the chapter 'Principles of Exposure'.

Underneath there are, as appropriate, LCD signals for focusing (red arrows, green dot) and flash-ready signals (red flash symbol) and on the right, a bright LCD field. The latter will display the set values (film speed, shutter speed, aperture, exposure correction) and letter symbols (automatic mode, manual mode) and other symbols (type of metering), some of which are also displayed on the data display panel on top of the camera. These displays will be described in detail under the chapters dealing with the use of the camera.

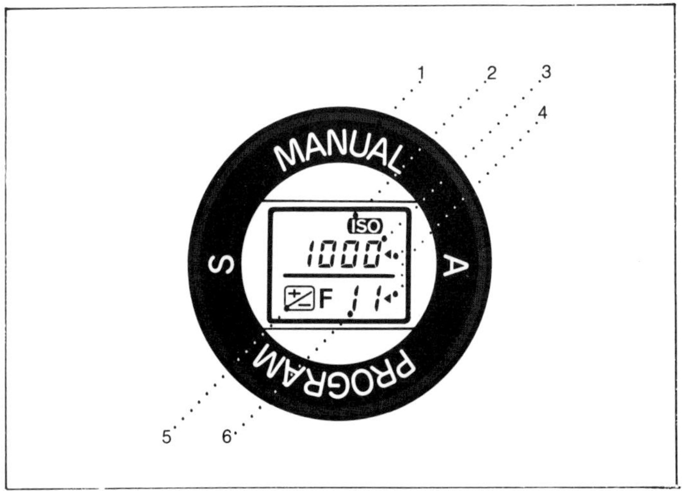

Sum total of all possible displays in the data field: **1** ISO marker, **2** signals that the group of numbers **3** represent the film speed (otherwise this would be shutter speed). The arrow points **4** point to the values selectable by the user, **5** is the exposure correction symbol, **6** the aperture or the correction value.

Short Photographic Guide

The Minolta 9000 is a highly sophisticated precision camera and as such should be used to its full potential. Fortunately it is not necessary to master everything at once, because one of the shooting modes available is the program mode; in this the 9000 will automatically take perfectly-exposed pictures, almost without the photographer's assistance. Despite the great variety of functions available, it is quite easy for the amateur to operate the camera. With increasing expertise it develops into an instrument for the professional.

To start the acquaintance it is a good idea to try out all its functions by a "dummy run", without loading any film. This will need some preparation: first, a lens will have to be attached (see "Lenses and Lens Changing" in the previous chapter) and suitable batteries need to be loaded.

Loading Suitable Batteries

Two size AA batteries, available almost everywhere (LR6, R6, AM3 or UM3 to mention only a few common descriptions) provide energy for all the Minolta 9000's circuits, except for the motor drive, flashgun and databack, which require their own batteries. Moreover, the Minolta 9000 may be described as "omniverous" in that any type of battery will do the job; alkaline, carbon-zinc or rechargeable nickel cadmium. That simplifies this particular aspect of camera handling. It is not necessary to employ special batteries such as silver oxide or lithium for special camera functions.

Inserting the batteries is just as simple. Set the camera in the OFF position and move the lever at the base of the camera in the direction of the arrow. Pull out

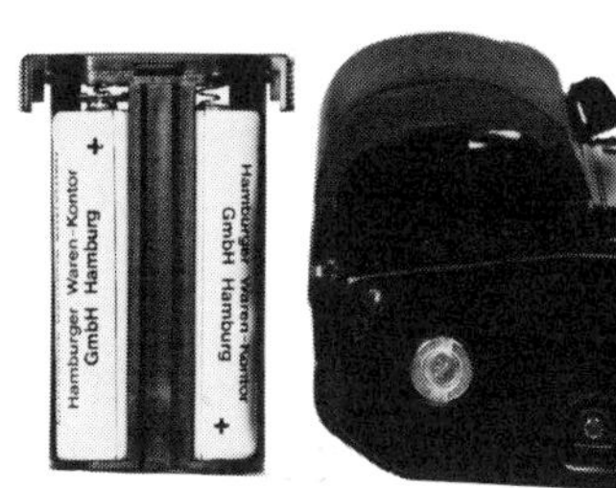

The two size AA batteries fit into the battery holder that can be pulled out of the handgrip.

the projecting end of the battery holder, insert the two batteries in the two compartments and push the holder into the handgrip until it engages. Spare battery holders are available for quick battery change-over.

The batteries enable the camera to retain some memory functions, even when it is switched off. For example, depending on the last-used shooting mode, the shutter speed or aperture setting used for the last shot and the film speed. In case of battery change, or re-insertion of a battery holder, the camera automatically sets the film speed by DX coding. If the inserted film has no DX codes, then the camera will indicate this by flashing "ISO 100" in the display, even if the camera is switched off. This is a warning that you have to set the film speed manually, refer to chapter "Camera and Film" under "automatic film speed setting").

Choice of Battery

The most convenient of all the available types of batteries are alkaline cells. They last longest and need to be replaced only when the entire LCD displays begin to flash (automatic battery test function). If you have a spare battery holder you simply insert it and replace the exhausted set in the holder later on. I usually carry an extra set of batteries in addition to a spare holder.

According to Minolta, a set of alkaline batteries will take about 60 films with 36 exposures each. This means a useful service of months, rather than days or weeks.

Rechargeable batteries are more economical, and they are also available in AA size. Their capacity runs to only 30 films, but they may be recharged over and over again. These nickel-cadmium rechargeable batteries are also suitable for low temperatures, but to carry a charger is not always convenient when travelling.

If need be, ordinary carbon-zinc batteries will do just as well. However, at best they will expose 20 films, and even fewer if they have been stored in the shop for a long period, which is often the case and collapse quickly as soon as they are nearly exhausted. This type therefore should only be used if no others are available.

The actual performance and effective life of every type of battery depends on the ambient temperature and other factors. For example, how fresh were the batteries when bought; within what period are they going to be be used? Low temperatures reduce the duration of use of carbon-zinc batteries in particular but to a lesser degree also alkaline batteries, whilst long storage periods affect zinc-carbon and also rechargeable batteries.

Further Preparations

All that now remains is to adjust the viewfinder eyepiece and secure the carrying strap.

The eyepiece adjustment is the small button to the left of the eyepiece. Remove the lens and hold the camera against a bright surface such as the sky or a white wall. Look through the viewfinder and turn the button until the

Snapshot with long focal length lens. To avoid camera shake the Minolta 9000 is set to shutter speed priority, with suitable preselected shutter speed.   *Photo: Hermine Gesteu*

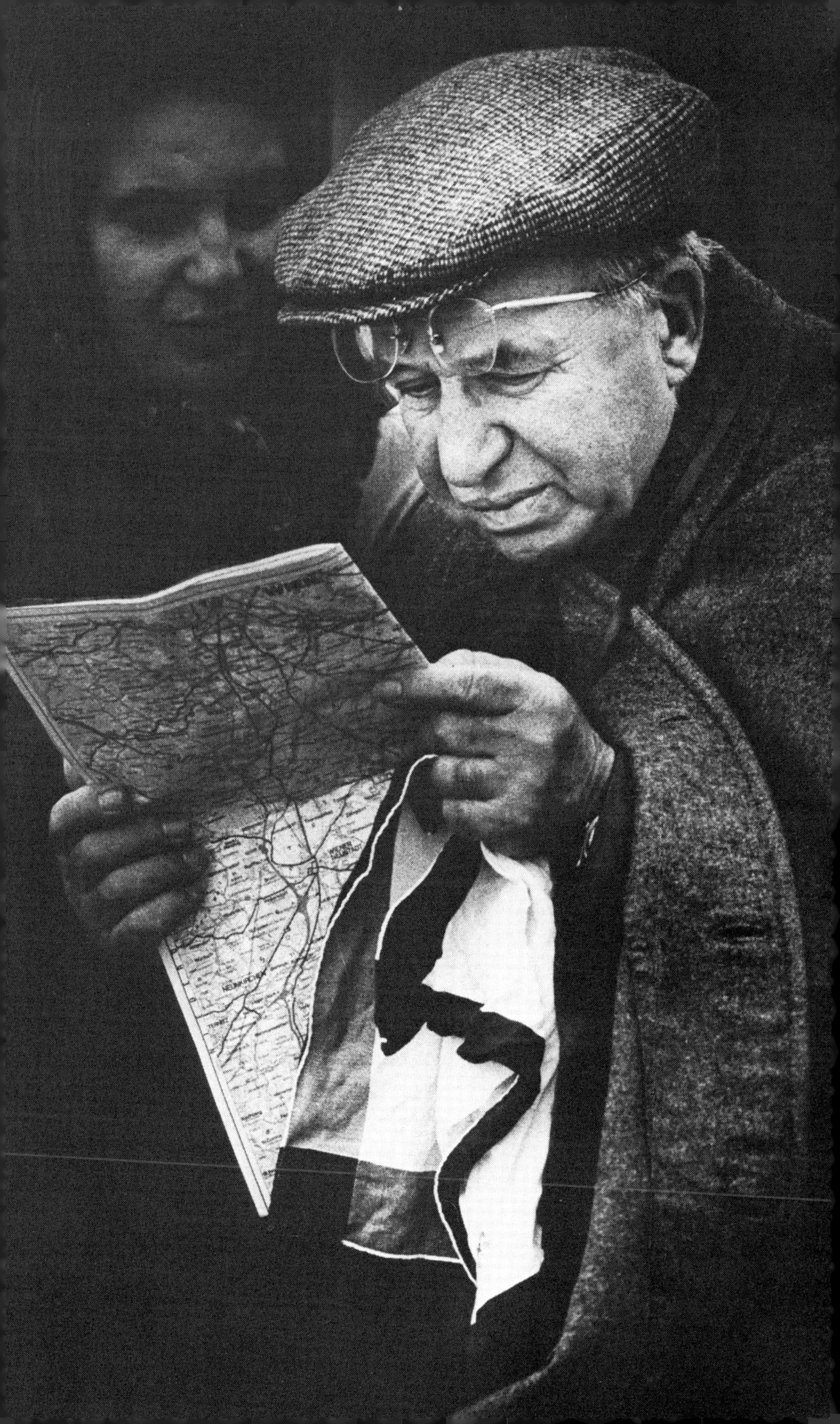

metering circle and the AF-target rectangle in the centre of the viewfinder appear sharpest. At this setting the image in the viewfinder will appear sharpest to you, even if the camera's automatic focusing takes care of this anyway. Those of you who wear glasses will have to decide whether you prefer to use the camera with or without glasses. I shall discuss this in more detail under the heading "Sharpness in the Viewfinder" in the chapter "Focusing Principles".

The carrying strap should also be attached at this point. Lead the end of the strap from top to bottom through the lugs on the side so that the rough anti-slip surface is on the inside of the strap, pointing towards the camera. The ends are then taken towards the outside through the buckles and upwards. The length can now be adjusted. A properly adjusted carrying strap is a valuable aid in supporting the camera correctly during shooting. In some cases it may be better to use the bottom lug on the left-hand side of the camera side (see also "Strap Support").

The Simplest Way: by Program

In order not to have to struggle with problems of exposure before you are sufficiently familiar with the camera, you may use the 9000's ability to take care of exposure automatically. This means you will have to turn the function switch until the legend PROGRAM engages above the triangular symbol. Push the main switch, at the right of the film advance lever, fully to ON and the audible warning symbol should now be visible. Set the AF switch to AF. Remove the lens cap and lightly touch

---

A telephoto lens in the close-up range allows the controlled use of the shallow depth of field in creating the desired effect.

Photo: Joachim F. Richter

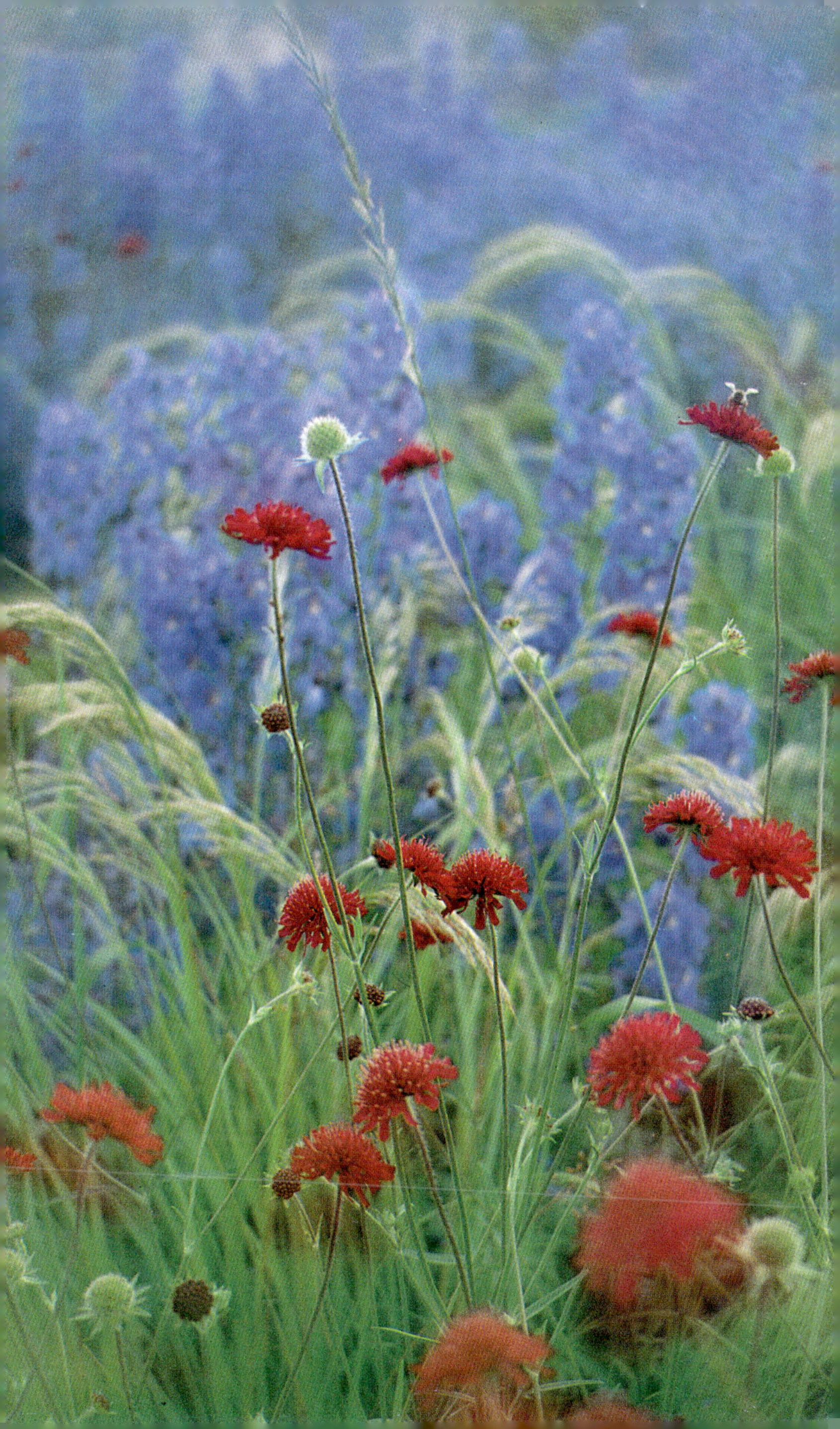

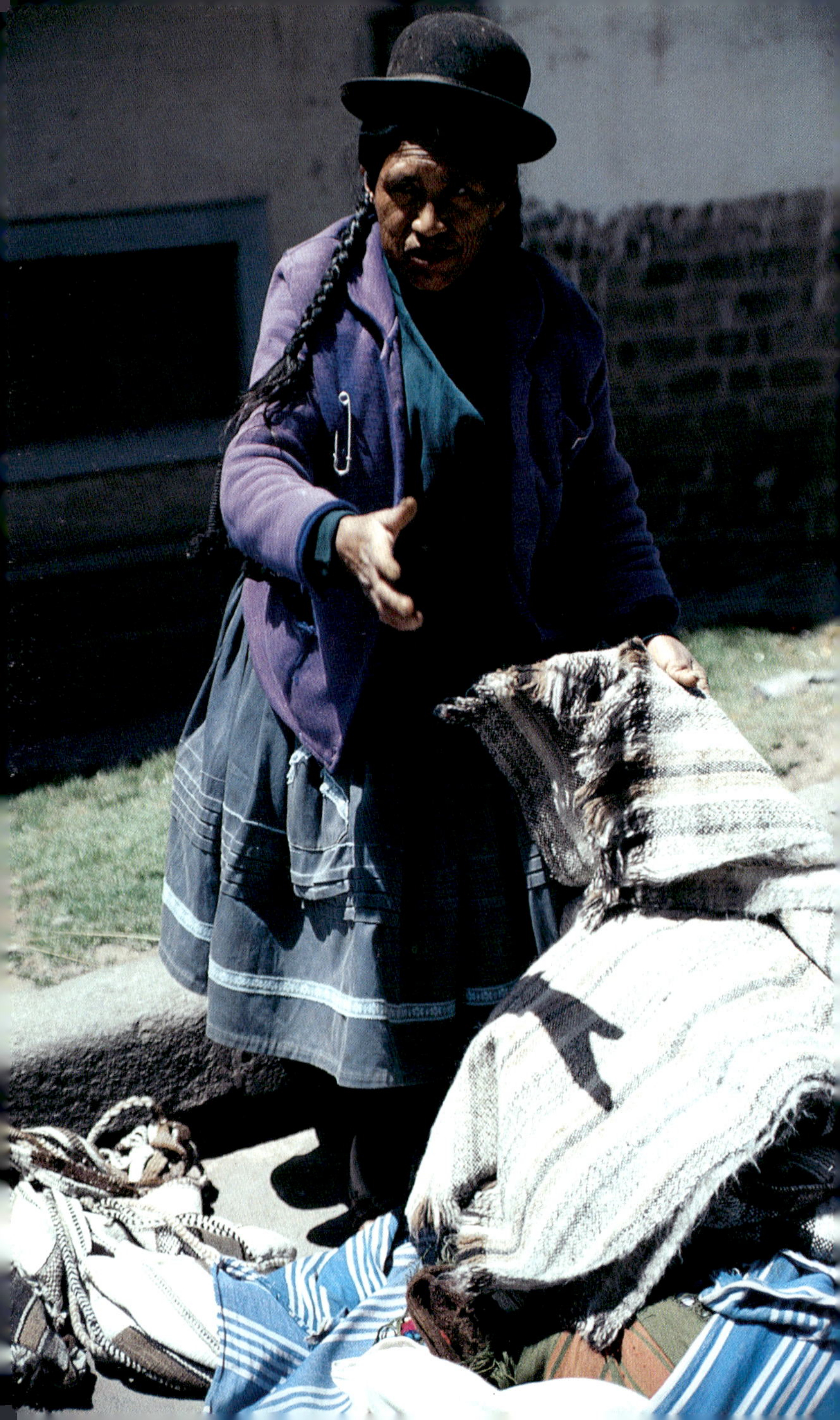

the release button, or tap it lightly if you are wearing gloves. A number will appear above the cross bar in the data display in the centre of the mode selector switch; this denotes the shutter speed, where 60 = $^1/_{60}$ second, below that is the f/number (aperture value). The same numbers (but without f/) will be indicated in the viewfinder at the bottom of the screen, to the right and left of the "P" symbol. If instead of the aperture value only "F - -" appears in the data display, then this indicates that no lens is attached!

The Test Run

You may do this without loading a film, but the camera has to be prepared as if a film were loaded. If the combination "4000" and "F22" appears in the data display, depress the release button and activate the film advance lever twice. This simulates two blank exposures, which are necessary after a film is loaded. Now turn the metering type selector (rewind button) until the white marker is opposite the legend AVERAGE. The subsequent manipulations are quite simple:

1. Point the camera at the important detail of the subject, the part which has to be in sharp focus, and locate it within the rectangular field where sharpness is measured.
2. Lightly tap the release button; the data display which had disappeared, reappears again and the focusing motor runs until a green circular indicator on the left under the viewfinder screen lights up (see also

For situation shots such as this Peruvian market woman in Cuzo there is not a lot of time to set up the shot. Good camera support and shortest possible shutter speed is of the utmost importance.

Photo: Joachim F. Richter

"manual focusing" for which the red arrow points light up). At the same time the object in the viewfinder will appear in sharp focus. The focusing motor will adjust the focusing so long as you keep your finger on the release button, either without exerting any pressure at all or only a slight pressure, and if the focused subject moves towards or away from the camera, or if you change the camera position by pointing it at a different object.

3. As soon as focusing is correct, depress the release button lightly. A bleeping sound confirms that the focus is now fixed; the motor will no longer adjust to focus on other objects in the frame.
4. Choose the actual framing if the sharpest part of the object is not supposed to be in the centre of the frame. The pressure on the release button must not be removed, otherwise the motor will start to re-focus again.
5. Now depress the release button fully. It is, of course, most important to hold the camera firmly and to support it if necessary.

Usually the five steps above are performed in one easy movement. Generally it will be the case of pointing the camera and pressing the release button as soon as the green signal indicates that everything is ready. What remains therefore is:

6. (starting from step 2) Switch forward. Move the film onto the next frame by moving the transport lever; this will cock the shutter at the same time. The transport lever may be activated in one movement (through 130°), or by several short strokes. One single stroke is faster. For some camera positions a few short strokes may be more comfortable as it may avoid the necessity to change one's hold on the camera.

The manipulations decribed above are not complicated. The same cannot be said about the functions they activate. What I have described is the automatic shooting mode which takes care of everything. You will see in the later chapters how you can influence the automatic shooting function and control certain aspects yourself. Another important factor in obtaining successful photographs is correct camera position and release.

Camera Shake

Using the auto-focusing facility and Minolta lenses, your pictures should be razor-sharp. Even so, sometimes you will find that your images are blurred. This is due to camera shake. The camera moved during the exposure. The longer the exposure time, the greater the danger of camera shake. Every slight movement during the time the shutter traverses the film plane will produce blurring of outlines.

One remedy to counteract camera shake is to keep the shutter speed as fast as possible. For hand-held shots the shutter speed should never be slower than $^1/_{125}$ second, i.e. the display shows "125". If the shutter speed is slower than $^1/_{125}$ second it means that the first interference in the program mode sequence has to be made. Place your right index finger on the time switch situated beneath the function switch and push it once or more to the left. Each time the switch is pushed the shutter speed is made faster by half a stop (e.g. from 60 to 90), therefore, pushing it twice will halve the time (display 60 to 125, i.e. $^1/_{60}$ to $^1/_{125}$ second). At the same time the aperture will open up by half a stop (e.g. from f/5.6 to f/4.5). The time may be reduced as long as larger aperture stops are available. When the shutter speed indicates $^1/_{30}$ second and the aperture has arrived at f/1.4, you may push the switch as often as you like, but the time cannot get any shorter. If the time switch is pulled towards the right, then the time is increased and the aperture size is decreased. The same may be achieved, in program mode, by pushing the aperture switch on the left of the lens up or down. This is discussed in more detail under the heading "Program Shift" in the chapter "Principles of Exposure".

If you have a reasonably steady hand you may expect sharp pictures for shutter speeds up to $1/125$ second. Longer times, perhaps necessary in poor lighting conditions, require special measures, otherwise it is almost certain that your pictures will be blurred.

Camera Support

Correct camera position also means comfortable camera position. If you are not entirely comfortable when supporting the camera, then you will not be able to hold it steady. Depending on the subject you are taking and on whether you rely entirely on the automatic focusing facility, you may hold the camera in one of various different ways.

First the simplest position, suitable for standard lenses and most other focal lengths. This is for shots in horizontal format, which is the handiest format as far as camera support is concerned. The right hand holds the camera, with the middle and ring fingers clasped around the hand grip on the right-hand side of the camera and the small finger supporting the base of the camera. The right thumb rests on the projection of the back panel beneath the transport lever, which is slightly folded out in its starting position; the right index finger rests on the release button. If the camera is switched on, the index finger also operates the AF setting. During the shot, the right index finger rests comfortably, ready for the two functions without having to change position: operation, possibly in conjunction with the thumb, of the function switch and of the previously mentioned time key. Other operating elements, e.g. main switch, are operated by the right hand before and after the shot.

Unlike other SLR cameras, the only function performed by the left hand is to support the camera; there are no aperture levers or setting rings that need to be operated. For those of you with small hands; the left hand holds the left side of the camera, the index and middle fingers at the front, the thumb along the lower edge of the back panel and the rest of the fingers, wherever they rest comfortably. My own big hands tend to be more comfortable by placing my left ring and little finger beneath the lens, with the middle finger resting on top and the index finger on the aperture key.

The knurled setting ring on the lens moves when the camera operates in AF mode, so take care not to interfere with this movement!

Which eye? It is easier with the right eye. You need not take your eye from the viewfinder eyepiece while transporting the film. If the sight in your left eye is better than in your right, then you will have to get used to the transport lever sticking into your right eye and will have to move the camera slightly off your face when transporting the film. This presents no problem, however, if you are using motor drive.

For upright format you swing the right hand up, the left supports the camera, retaining its position, especially if the middle and ring fingers are already placed around the lens. This is perfectly all right for the occasional upright shot. For longer sequences in this format it may be better to reposition the left hand by placing the left thumb on the camera top (prism housing) and the other fingers against the now vertical camera base. The camera now rests securely and naturally in the left hand.

When taking pictures in upright format it is definitely more comfortable to view with the right eye because in this position the right thumb is well supported against the front and the camera back against the nose.

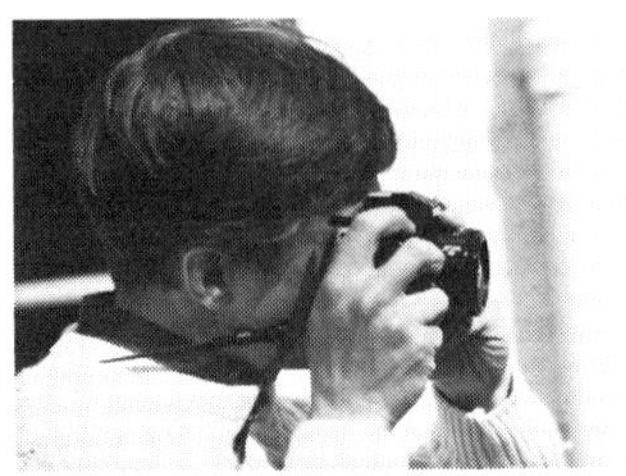

Normal camera position for horizontal format with fixed focal length lenses. The position of the left hand is particularly suitable for people with large hands.

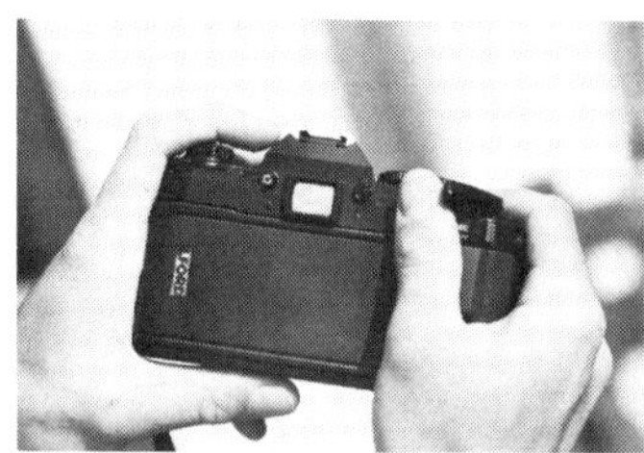

Position of thumbs at the back of the camera: the right thumb on the back panel below the angled transport lever, the left below the bottom edge.

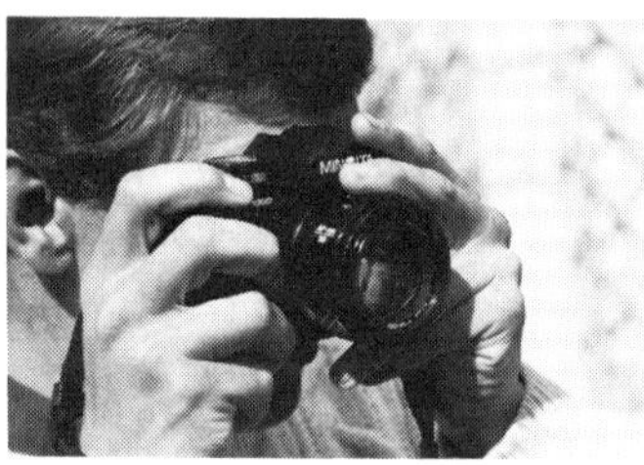

The camera is quickly lifted to the eye, the strap leading across the shoulder is now tight (if it is correctly adjusted), affording extra support. The other end of the strap is attached to the lower lug in this position.

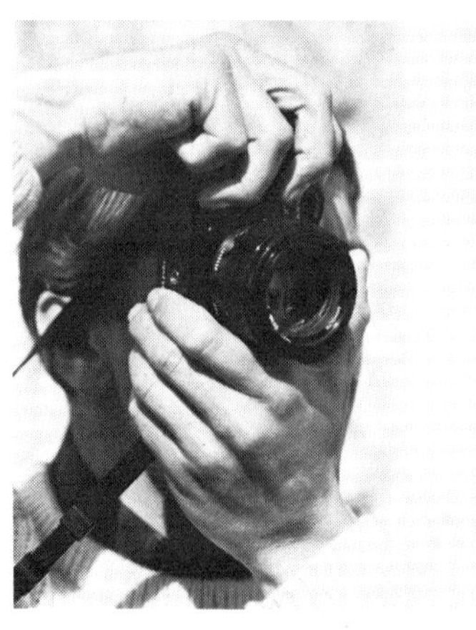

The best position for upright format is by supporting the camera with the left hand, with fingers reaching round the lens. Using the left eye would enable one to support the camera even better against the forehead.

It is best to follow these instructions and to try them out a few times. You will soon find out what your own particular preferences are and where to put the fingers that are not actually needed to perform any particular function.

With Zoom Lenses

Manipulating a zoom lens, i.e. a lens with variable focal length, requires a slightly different holding position with the left hand. When taking horizontal format shots, the ring and the little fingers support the camera from beneath, whilst the thumb and the middle finger, and for very long lenses perhaps even the index finger also, turn the zoom ring. Again, care must be taken that the other fingers, index finger in case of a 35-70mm lens and ring finger for 28-135mm lenses, do not obstruct the movement of the setting ring.

The most compact of the range, the 35-70mm f/4 zoom lens affords the most comfortable holding position; with all the others it is necessary to move the hand forward to operate the zoom ring.

For upright format start again with the usual position, right thumb on top of camera, the rest of the fingers pressed against the base, but now reach forward with thumb and index or middle finger to find the zoom ring.

A good stance is also very important. If possible support yourself against a wall, a tree, or whatever may be available. If there is no suitable support, spread your legs and support your elbows against your chest. Or support your elbows on some railings, a wall, a table top, the back of a chair. If you are sitting on the ground, your bent knees could provide excellent support. Always remember, the better the support the more likely is a blur-free result.

Further aids are, of course, table- or full-size tripods.

For further description turn to the chapter headed "Tripods".

On the other hand to support yourself on, or to lean against, rigid fittings in moving vehicles is not recommended. It is exactly those movements that we try to counteract. It is best to stand freely, perhaps with slightly bent knees, to make your body act as a sort of shock absorber. This applies in particular to shots from a boat, train, plane, helicopter or other vehicles. Some professional photographers construct special vibration absorbing camera straps if they are often called upon to take shots under such circumstances.

Using the Strap as Support

The camera strap serves not only to carry the camera, it can be used to help support the camera during shooting. For the quick shot it is necessary to have the camera always at the ready. There are several ways:
O   The camera is worn, hanging from the strap around

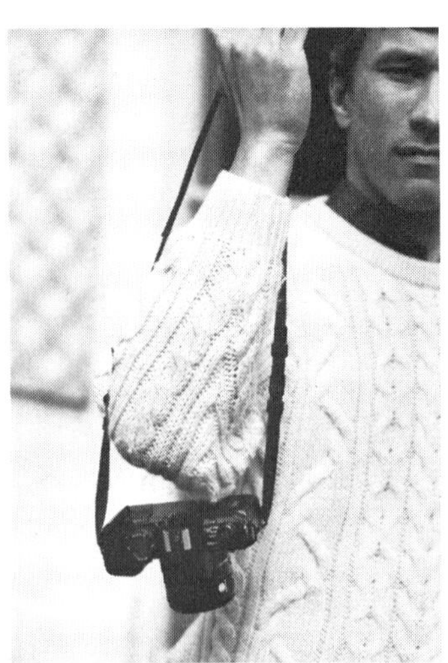

Correct length of strap for carrying camera around the shoulder. Held in this way the camera should hang just below the elbow. It is better to have the strap fixed to the left lower lug.

the neck. It may be quickly and easily moved to the eye, but the photographer, or perhaps the eager snap-happy tourist is easily recognised as such.

○ A less obvious position is to carry the camera with the strap on the right shoulder, but this is less safe. The camera is better protected if it is carried under the jacket; it is well concealed up to the last moment and is still easily accessible. Only if you carry it with a large lens attached is this method not very convenient. Carried in this fashion it is better to thread the strap through the lower lug rather than the upper.

○ Carrying the camera with its strap around the neck and obliquely across the chest is a very safe way and is a precaution also against its being torn away or theft. In this position it cannot slip and is easily moved to the eye. The Minolta strap is tear-proof.

The length of the strap should be adjusted so that it affords good support in normal camera shooting positions, whilst at the same time it is comfortable for carrying and hanging round the neck. One general rule

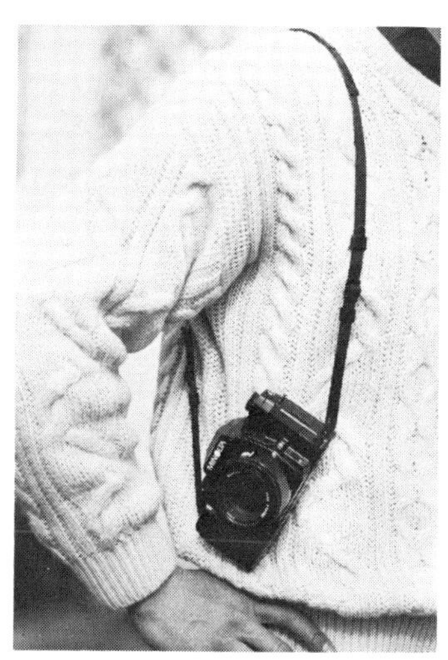

The camera carried around the right shoulder, it is always ready and can even be worn under the jacket, but only with the smaller lenses.

applies to both cases; suspend the camera from your thumb and stretch your arm straight upwards. The strap would be of about correct length when the camera hangs just below elbow height.

If you prefer to carry the camera under one arm, over one shoulder, then the length of the strap will have to be increased. Adjust the length so that when the camera is raised to the eye, the strap leads from the left, lower lug across the left shoulder, across the back and below the right arm, ending in the angle of the right hand at the right lug. The strap will be taut when pushing the right arm down and the head forward against the camera: head, camera and right hand then form a solid unit. However, this position is not so good for shots in upright format, and the strap would have to be lengthened.

If the camera is worn around the neck, you should first wrap the strap around your right wrist before lifting it to the eye. The left hand reaches from the left and top across the strap, which is attached to the top lug in this case, and the strap is further wrapped around the left wrist, to produce a tight, but comfortable support around the neck. Again, camera, head and hands form a rigid unit.

Even easier to lift to shooting position is the camera that is worn around the right shoulder. In this case the strap runs from the right side of the camera, underneath the armpit, forward across the shoulder, past the face to the left, lower lug. Again, the strap leading tightly across arm and shoulder will present a good support for the camera in shooting position. In all these cases it is important that the length of the strap is correctly adjusted. I would suggest that you try all these positions and choose the one best suited to you. The strap may then be adjusted and left in this, the most comfortable position.

As mentioned previously, the camera hanging around one shoulder, underneath a jacket, is a secure way of carrying it. It will be necessary, though, to take at least one arm out of the jacket to hang the camera around the shoulder. It is also possible to get straps in two parts with snap hook fasteners which would be quite useful in this case. However these cannot be easily attached to the strap-fastening mechanism on the Minolta 9000. Perhaps you could devise your own solution.

Releasing the Shutter

A good camera position alone will not ensure that one's pictures are free from the effects of camera shake. The camera also has to be kept steady during shutter release.

The release button of the Minolta 9000 has several functions: a light touch will switch on the light meter and the focusing mechanism. A slight pressure suffices if you are wearing gloves or your hands are very dry; depressing the key by 0.4mm will activate the same switch.

Depressing the key further to a total of about 0.7mm fixes the focusing setting. Depressing the key fully (a further 0.4mm) will release the shutter. This last operation is the important part. The electric switch, being activated by the pressure on the button, has a soft, but still noticeable pressure point after about 1mm. A very slight pressure will suffice to trigger the shutter as soon as focusing is fixed.

The safest method is to hold the hand grip firmly and to place the entire last joint of the index finger on the upper surface. The finger joint on the self timer switch and the tip of the finger on the release key. The first finger joint creates the pressure to depress the button. This is best practised with the camera switched off, as you can get the feel of how much pressure to exert in order to overcome the pressure point, and how to perform this while keeping the camera absolutely steady.

When the release is activated and the camera switched

on, the viewfinder image will disappear for the duration of the exposure time but this is hardly noticeable at fast shutter speeds. This is when the mirror folds away and then returns again into position. If, at this point the button is released, the LCD beneath the viewfinder will disappear. Touching the release button again will reactivate the viewfinder image for another 10 seconds.

How long the release button is kept depressed has no influence on the exposure time, and it may be released as soon as the mirror is folded away. The only exception is when using the BULB exposure setting in manual mode. In this case the shutter will remain open as long as the button is held depressed (see also chapter headed "Principles of Exposure").

Holding your breath for the duration of making the exposure should also help in keeping the camera as steady as possible. However, I would not recommend taking a deep breath and trying to hold it for any length of time. This could have quite the opposite effect. It is also advisable to stop and calm yourself should you be out of breath in the attempt to catch a particular shot. If possible take a minute or two to catch your breath after you climbed that steep hill.

And finally, always move the film onto the next frame after taking a shot: activate the transport lever in several short or one long stroke and then allow it to return to the starting position. This will cock the shutter for the next shot and the frame counter will advance to the next number or dot; these alternate. It is possible to cock the shutter without moving the film, a technique which is used to get certain effects; two or more exposures on one and the same frame (see also "Multiple Exposures" in the chapter "Principles of Exposure").

Using a Tripod

If you have a steady hand and are experienced in

releasing the shutter, it is generally possible to achieve sharp images with shutter speeds as slow as $^1/_{125}$ second with standard and wide-angle lenses. Using supports of various kinds it is even possible to achieve good results with hand-held shots at speeds of $^1/_{30}$ second. I have known some particularly steady types who could hand-hold their camera at $^1/_6$ second. Whatever your own ability may be, a tripod is definitely better.

If you are using a large and heavy telephoto lens, such as the AF Apo 300mm f/2.8 and the 600mm f/4, it will be essential to use a good professional tripod and not one of those light ones with thin legs. This not only keeps the camera firmly supported during the shot, but also pointing at the correct section of subject that the very narrow viewing angles of these extreme lenses allow. Apart from these special applications, which call for a tripod as an essential part of the equipment, it is usually inconvenient to carry one and we have to look round for some other form of support.

I usually carry a table-top tripod with tilt top which can be accomodated in the gadget bag (such as the TR-1 by Minolta). This is useful for positioning the camera with moderate telephoto and zoom lens (70-210mm or 75-300mm) on a suitable base (table, wall, balustrade, etc.), ensuring that the camera is sufficiently rigid, even for long exposure times.

Such a table-top tripod can also be used as a chest support. Attach the camera to the ball and socket head so that the eyepiece fits comfortably to the eye. If the whole assembly is pressed tightly to the body during the shot, then it is possible to obtain sharp images for speeds down to $^1/_{30}$ second. This is a useful aid on sports grounds, at the circus or any other location where you are forced to take your photographs from a seat and need to use the longer lenses.

For interior shots with wide-angle to average telephoto lenses, in churches for example, I usually support the camera on a small tripod against a wall or a column. I am able to achieve sharp images even with long exposures.

Self-Timer

The Minolta 9000 offers the facility for releasing the shutter with a 10 seconds delay. This is done by an electronic self-timer the switch of which is situated on the right of the release button. Push the switch to the right (a red strip becomes visible), then depress the release button. The red LED at the front flashes at a rate of two times per second during the first eight seconds, then eight times in the ninth second, in the tenth the LED remains illuminated. If switched on, the bleep signal will sound at the same rate. It is possible to interrupt this sequence at any time and to switch over to normal release, or to start again.

I find the self-timer rather inconvenient for the usual applications such as self-portraits and groups which include the photographer. It's not exactly ideal to run like a madman from the camera to the subject position before

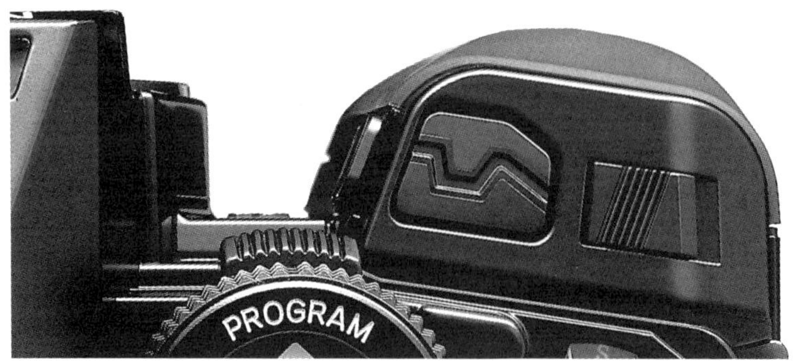

For self-timer shots push the self-timer button outward and then the release. The LED blinks slowly at first, then faster and remains illuminated for the last second of the countdown.

the shutter releases. The Minolta 9000 offers some much more elegant solutions with remote release RC-1000S or RC-1000L (described in chapter "Motor Drive and Control Functions") which offers the facility to decide the exact moment of taking the shot. It is also possible to do this by infra-red remote control 1R-1N, but in this case at the cost of doing without the automatic focusing facility.

The self-timer is useful for slow shutter speeds to ensure release free of shake, either on a tripod or even for supported, hand-held shots. In that case you can concentrate on getting as good a support as possible without having to worry about steady releasing as well. This comes in useful in poorly-lit situations, as for example, in churches, where I use a table-top tripod braced against a wall (see "Tripod Support").

Manual Focusing

The automatic focusing facility works perfectly for almost all subjects, as long as they are not too dark or lack detail. For various reasons (see "Principles of Sharpness") it fails under certain circumstances. Luckily, it will notify you if that is the case. If, after a focusing attempt, two inward pointing arrows light up instead of the green dot marker, then this means that the subject conditions are unsuitable for electronic focusing. In such a case it will be necessary to focus manually. Push the switch at the bottom next to the lens, so that it uncovers "M" and covers "AF". Then reach with your left hand slightly forward for the knurled lens setting ring, which is turned until the object appears in sharp focus in the viewfinder. You may have to turn a little towards the right and then to the left to find the point of optimum sharpness. It is difficult to obtain exact focusing in poor lighting conditions, which may have been the reason why the electronic autofocus was unable to achieve satisfactory setting.

For manual focusing the camera is held a little differently. The left hand supports the camera with ring and little finger from below, thumb and index (or middle) finger turn the focusing ring.

The red arrow points may be ignored in manual focusing. However, if the green dot does light up, then you are assured that the target object in the metering rectangle is correctly focused. This could happen if, for example, more light falls on the subject.

Choice and Use of Lenses

I would like to mention one thing straight away: it may be better to attach a zoom lens to the Minolta 9000, rather than one of the standard 50mm lenses that are usually offered when buying a camera. Particularly attractive is the AF 35-70mm f/4 that, hardly any heavier or larger than the usual fixed focus 50mm f/1.4, lends extra dimension to your image creation.

The use of such a lens allows change of scale and framing, without having to change position. Turning the oblique zoom ring to the right will make the image appear larger in the viewfinder, but less of the subject will fit into the frame. Turning the ring to the left will bring in a wider section of the view presented to the camera (a wider angle). The use of the zoom setting soon becomes second nature, just as pointing the camera: sight the subject, turn the zoom ring and release

Fast film loading and reliable film transport is essential, particularly on expensive foreign trips. The Minolta 9000 even satisfies heavy professional use. The view opposite shows an archeological excavation at Machu Picchu in Peru. *Photo: Joachim F. Richter*

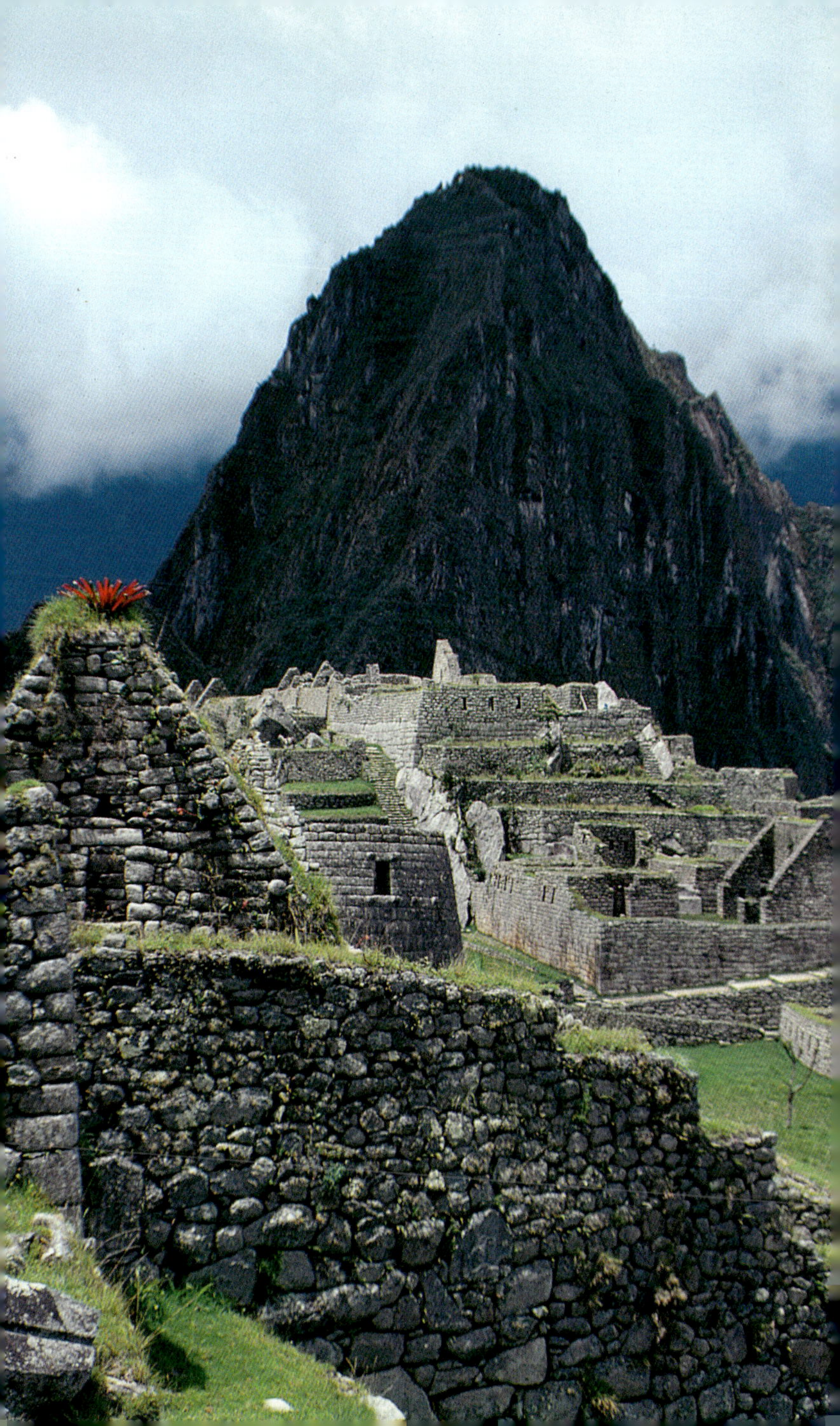

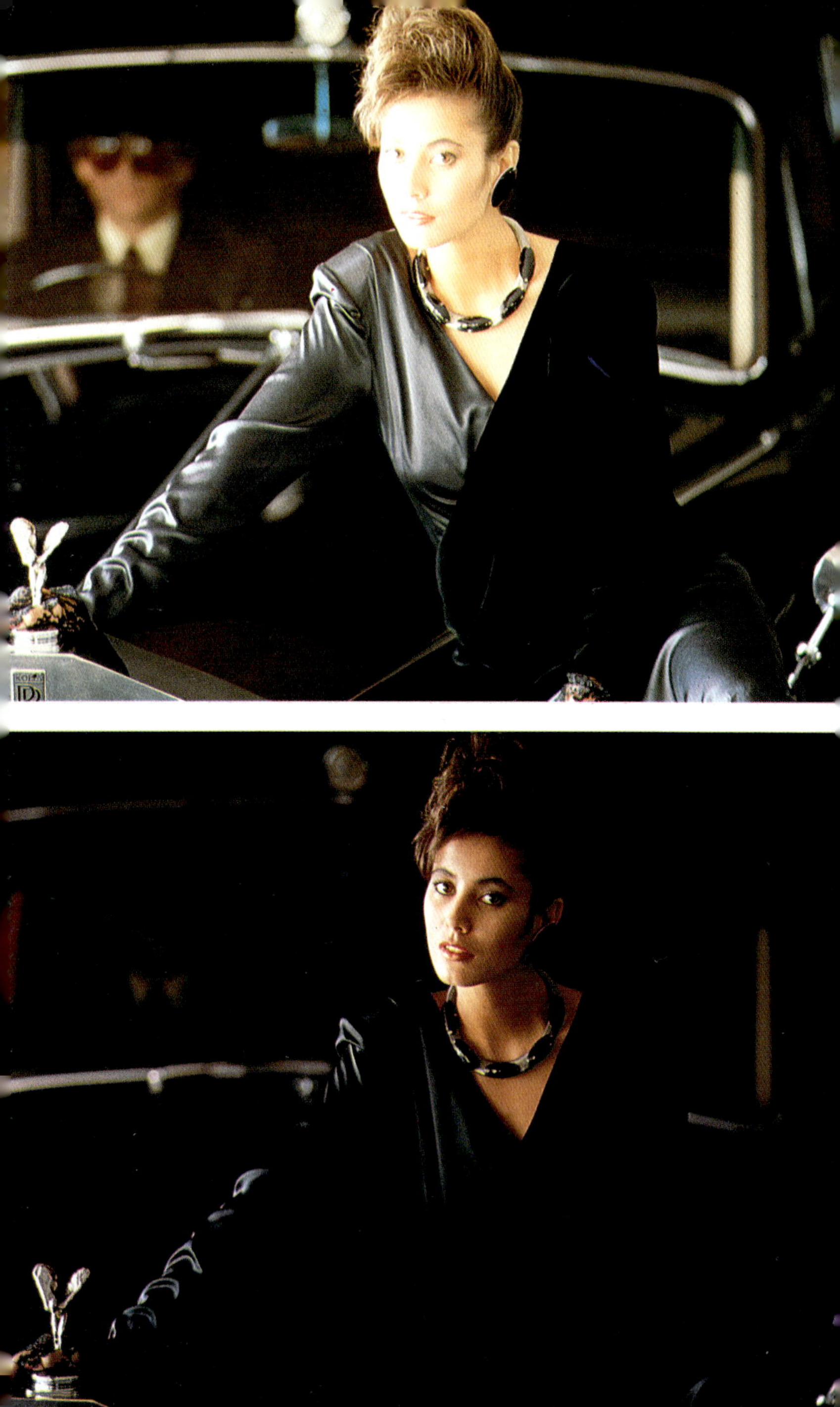

the shutter as soon as the green marker appears, indicating that focusing is correct.

Better focusing accuracy is achieved by allowing the electronic focusing function to act with the important subject detail at the telephoto setting, the subject appearing large in the metering area, and then turning the zoom ring to the required framing. This requires a little more time and is therefore not always practicable.

My favourite zoom is the 28-85mm, although this lens is a little larger and heavier than the standard lens. It allows the picture frame section to be considerably extended in both directions (zoom ratio 3:1 against 2:1 of the 35-70mm). But the principle of control and handling is the same.

In predominantly dark situations the automatic exposure mode will overexpose the shot, the bright areas will appear washed out (top). Better results are achieved by reducing the exposure. This may be done by spotmetering a characteristic shady section (metering type selector to S). The dark mood should not be confused with poor lighting which is automatically accounted for by the electronic metering, sometimes both situations coincide.

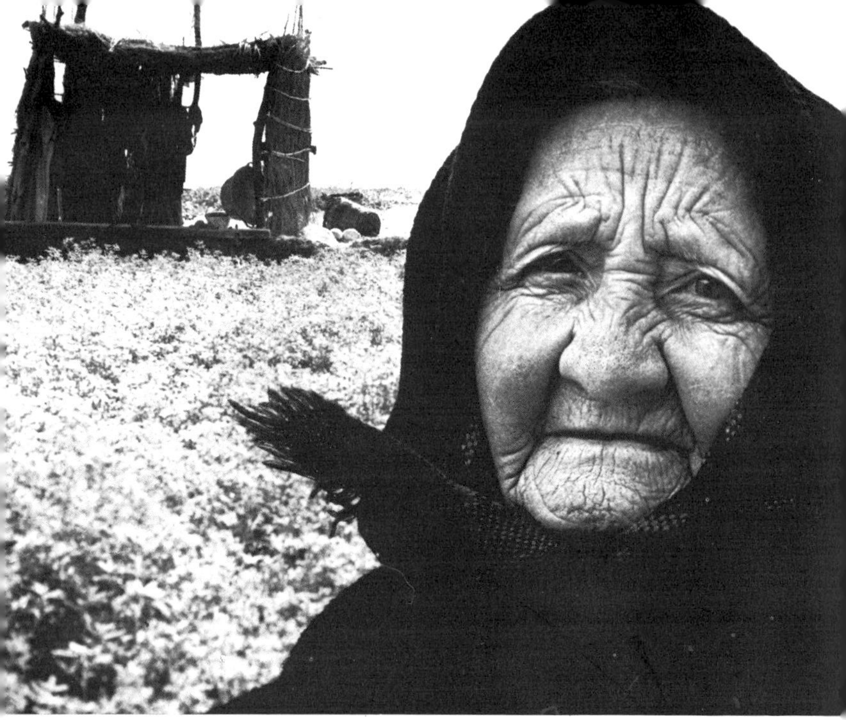

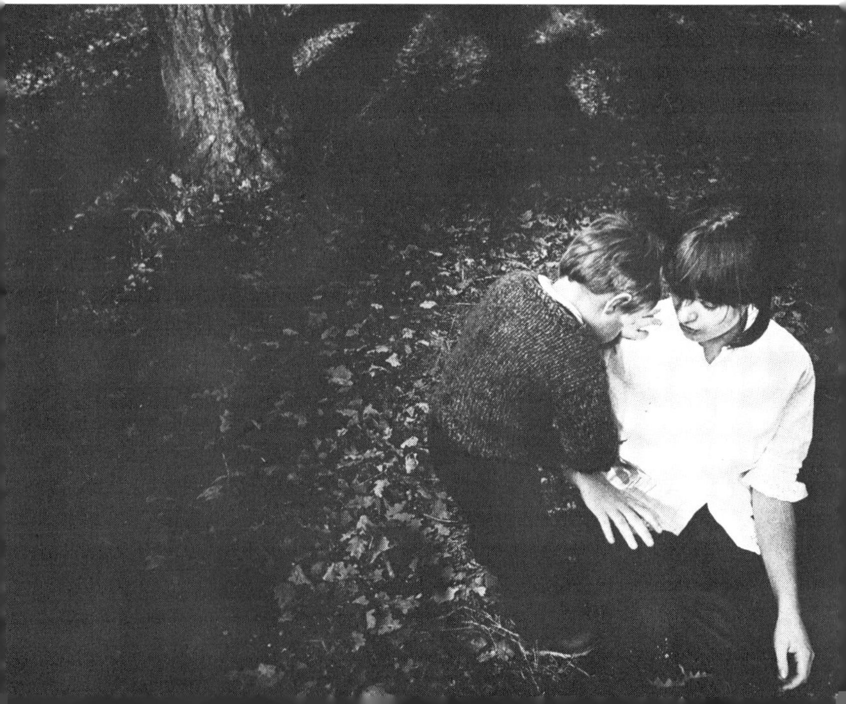

Camera and Film

The Minolta 9000 uses the most common type of 35mm film which is available almost everywhere in standard cassettes of up to 36 frames. This standardization was decided on almost by accident about 50 years ago and has been retained despite repeated suggestions for improvement. This is mainly due to marketing policies and not technological reasons. It is rather cumbersome as the film has to be carefully threaded, wound and correctly aligned and, after use, the entire 1.6m of film has to be rewound into the cassette.

Loading The Film

Loading the film quickly and safely is a procedure which takes a little practice. You would be well advised to buy a cheap film (24 exposures) and to practise with it as often as necessary until you can do it blindfolded, which you may be called upon to do some day. By the way, never load the film in direct sunlight, at least turn round and work in your own shadow. This is what you have to do:

1. Open camera back.
2. Insert cassette into film compartment.
3. Hook end of film into take-up spool.
4. Turn film a little way round the spool and then tighten with rewind crank.
5. Close camera back.
6. Advance film to first frame (No.1) and, if appropriate, set film speed.

Because of its abstracting effect many photographers use black-and-white film as their creative medium. The modern ISO 400 films with their excellent resolution and fine grain produce good results even in poor lighting conditions.

The Camera Back

The back panel of the Minolta 9000 has double security. The back panel lock is coupled to the rewind crank. To open; lift the crank, hold it, push the black safety catch, immediately in front of the crank, in the direction of the arrow and pull the crank fully up. The back panel will now open.

The cassette compartment with a series of six double contacts for sensing film speed is inside on the left; on the right is the take-up spool with the slots. The transport roller immediately to the left of the spool moves the film along by its perforations. In the centre is the focal register, closed by the shutter. The shutter blades, which are extremely thin leaves of light metal, are the most delicate accessible parts of the camera. Under no circumstances should these be touched! The least distortion in their shape would render the shutter completely useless.

The two pairs of polished tracks above and below the frame window, together with the black film pressure-plate, form a channel that ensures correct position of the film when the back is closed.

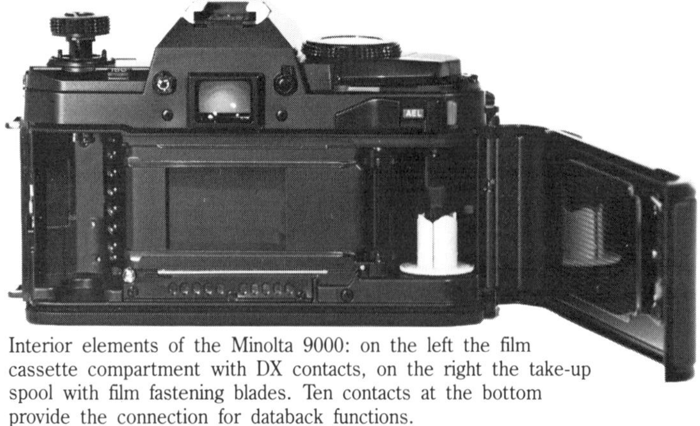

Interior elements of the Minolta 9000: on the left the film cassette compartment with DX contacts, on the right the take-up spool with film fastening blades. Ten contacts at the bottom provide the connection for databack functions.

When opening the camera for the first time you will find a thin protective foil which should be removed, if it doesn't fall out of its own accord.

The film window for reading the film data is built into the back panel. This window is framed in foam to protect the camera interior against incident light. The back panel may be exchanged for a databack (see also chapter "Motordrive and Control Functions"); ten contacts beneath the film track are provided for the necessary transfer of data.

Securing The Film

To insert the film cassette, the rewind crank and with it the rewind spindle inside, has to be fully pulled out. The cassette is inserted in the compartment on the left, the

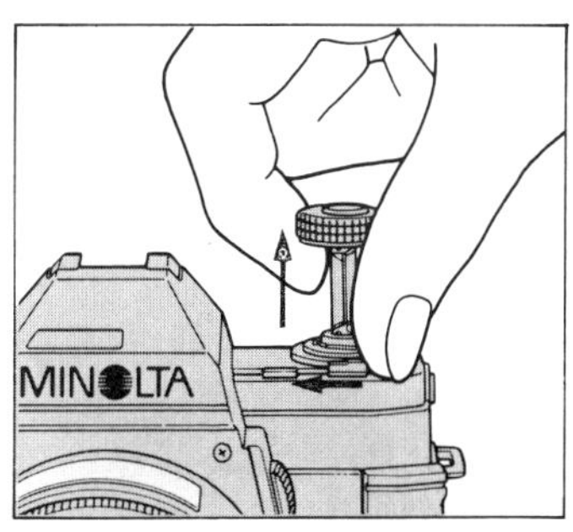

When loading the film the leader has to be inserted from right to left under one of the spool blades (below right).

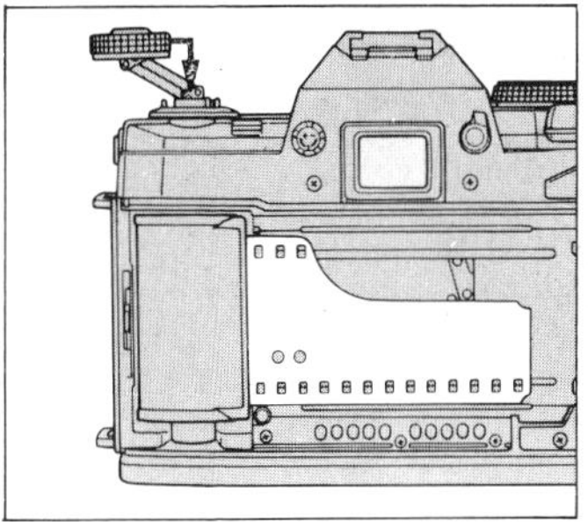

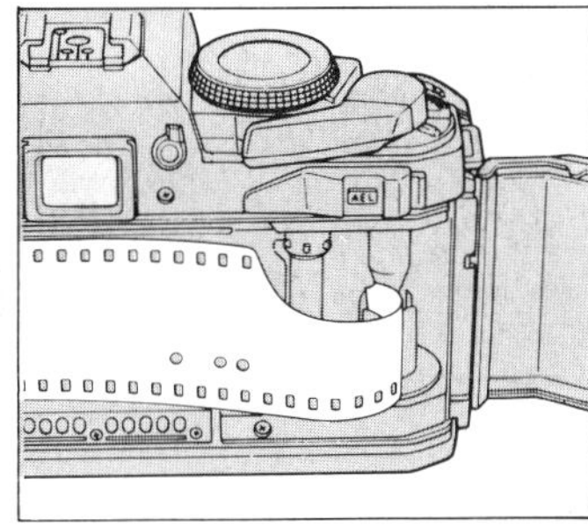

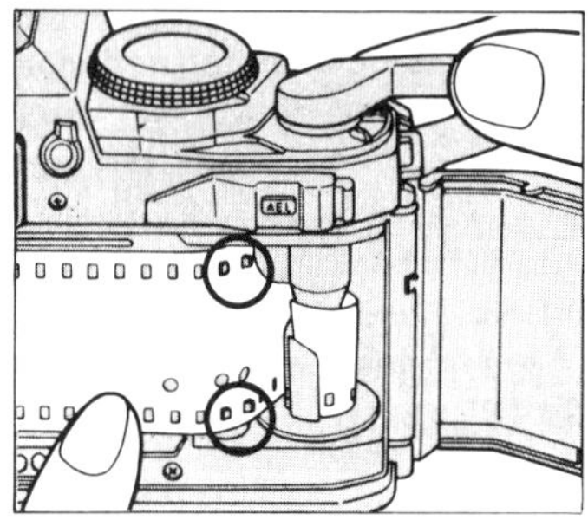

Correct film feeding: the film should lie flat and the perforations top and bottom should engage the sprockets; the back may then be closed.

projecting head of the spool facing down and the free film end pointing to the right. Now the crank may be pushed in and turned to ensure that the spool is completely engaged.

Now take the end of the film and pull it across, over the focal register, to the right-hand side until the curved end can be inserted in one of the slits on the take-up spool. The correct fixing of the film in the spool is most important. The film must not be inserted straight from left to right and then be hooked under one of the white slits of the take-up spool. This is the correct procedure with other cameras, but incorrect with the Minolta 9000. Here the film has to be bent round the reel from right to left, running into one of the slits, and making sure it does not lead out of another one. This is the only way the film will wind properly without kinking. If the spool support is now turned by hand one of the little teeth will hook into the perforations of the film and move it along.

If the film is incorrectly loaded it may still be possible to move it. But when it comes to winding it back into the cassette it may break as the initial length does not move easily out of the spool. The real danger is that tiny splinters of film may be loose inside the camera and could then damage delicate parts, such as the shutter.

As mentioned above, the spool support is turned from right to left until the start of the film is wound around the reel with emulsion side outwards. Turn a little further until the perforations engage on both sides of the transport roller. The rewind crank is again pulled upwards, without unlocking the back panel catch, and turned in the direction of the arrow until the film lies straight and tight on its track. Now press the back panel firmly home and push the rewind crank back.

The portion of the film that was exposed to the light during loading is now wound on until a fresh section appears in the focal register.

Now switch on the main switch and lightly touch the release button. 4000/F22 will be displayed in the data display. Depress the release button and advance film by the transport lever until No.1 appears in the frame counter and the film speed is displayed instead of 4000/F22. Another slight pressure will display the currently set aperture and shutter speed combination.

Film Trimming

The film end protruding from the cassette is usually cut to a 2cm wide and 4-5cm long strip which makes it easier to insert the end into the take-up spool. It may be that the perforations get damaged when trying out film loading. This should present no great problem. Simply cut off the end and cut a new tapered section, it need not follow the original shape, it suffices that the film is cut at an angle so that the lower edge has about three perforations more than the top edge.

Film Indexing

The film speed is an important factor in determining the correct exposure and this value has to be entered either manually or automatically when loading the film.

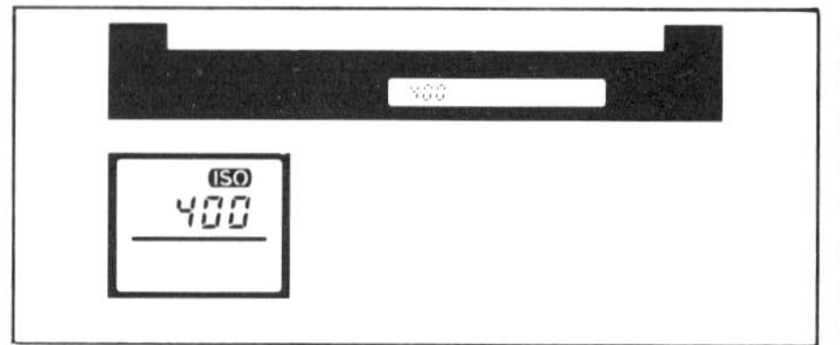

After the two blank shots the ISO display of film speed appears in the data display and in the viewfinder. Using cassettes without DX-coding the film speed has to be adjusted manually.

Automatic: modern film cassettes of most makes bear a coded film speed indication, the black and white strips. The contacts in the cartridge compartment sense the electrically conductive fields and the camera's electronics interpret the codes as the appropriate film speed value for exposure calculation.

This is done quite automatically when the film is loaded. After advancing the two blind shots the film speed display appears, "ISO" and a number above the line of the LCD field on top of the camera, and the film speed value alone on the left in the viewfinder LCD panel. This disappears again after slightly depressing the release. Now the setting is controllable. When the camera is switched on and the ISO key is depressed, then the value of the film speed of the film loaded at the time will be displayed. Releasing the key will return the metering control function and display for the usual ten seconds.

Manually: If a film without DX-coding is loaded, the last set film speed value will appear after the two blind shots. If this value is not correct for the new film, then it has to be adjusted. Depress the ISO key and keep it depressed. At the same time push the speed key as often to the left to increase film speed, or to the right to decrease film speed, until the correct value is displayed. If the speed key is kept pushed over, the values will adjust continually, either in an increasing or a decreasing sequence depending on the direction.

The same procedure may be adopted for adjusting the

film speed read automatically by the camera. You may wish to do this in certain situations to influence development characteristics of the entire film, in fact this would be equivalent to an exposure correction of the entire film.

The DX-coding covers values from 25 to 5000. The manual ISO setting range ranges from 6 to 6400. This has no practical implications as there are no films with speeds above ISO 5000 or below 25.

Manual re-adjustment of the film speed for film without DX-coding is also necessary after changing the batteries and after removal and re-insertion of the battery holder. In this case "ISO 100" will blink in the display and "100" in the viewfinder until the ISO key is depressed. A single depression will select ISO 100 as film speed, or the new value may be set as previously described. If a DX-coded cartridge is loaded the value will be automatically reset; only special adjustments have to be repeated.

The speed of the loaded film may be checked through the film window at the back of the camera. Most types of film show the film speed, and also sometimes the type of film and number of exposures. This information may be read through the film window.

Unloading the Film

When the film has been fully exposed it has to be rewound into its light-tight cassette before being removed. You can feel that the film is used up because the transport lever cannot be advanced any further. Do not force it across, as this would break the perforations and, as mentioned before, tiny fragments of film could cause a lot of damage inside the camera. You should also keep a watch on the frame counter (e.g. the red 36 or 24), particularly if you feel some resistance against the

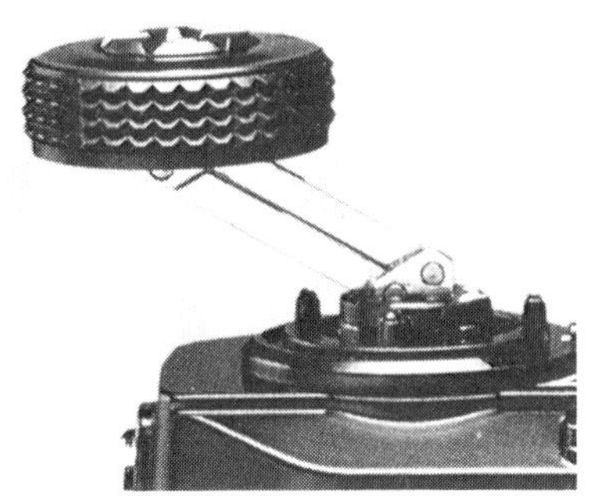

movement of the transport lever.

If you send your film to one of the large labs for processing you will be well advised to consider the last exposure on the film as lost. If you are loading a new film straight away you could repeat that last shot, just to be on the safe side. The reason for this lies in the fact that the large processing labs usually join the individual films together in long strips to feed them into the automatic developing machines. Any exposure that is close to the end of a film could therefore be spoilt by the joining tape.

The rewind crank of the Minolta 9000 is a little unusual: it has to be pulled up and then moved sideways to form a crank, in which position it is very easy to operate. In its completely retracted state it becomes the selector key for exposure modes. The crank knob wobbles a little during turning. This is intentional as it is easier to operate.

Manual rewinding is easy but slow. Fully depress the release button at the bottom of the camera, lift the rewind crank (but do not touch the back panel release at this point) and unfold it. Now turn it in the direction of the arrow until you feel a slight resistance, at which point the film end is released from the take-up spool, turn another three or four revolutions. Now pull the crank fully up and release the back panel lock. Open the back panel and remove the fully rewound cassette, but not in direct sunlight.

It is advisable to keep the film in a light-tight container. This need not necessarily be the original container. I usually use the boxes in which some labs return developed slides. Covered in black adhesive tape these give excellent protection and can hold about four films. When passing security checks at airports I usually put these containers in my pockets to avoid passing my films thorough the X-ray machines, which are often harmful. Posso supply similar containers for three film cassettes. These plastic containers contain a certain proportion of heavy metal and are supposed to afford some protection against X-rays, even so, I still prefer to protect them on my person.

Following the above procedure will completely retract the film into the cassette. You will know straight away that this is an exposed film and will not make the mistake of reloading an already exposed film. However, it is also impossible to reload a partially exposed film if the film end has been completely rewound in this manner. If you wish to leave the end of the film protruding, which also makes it slightly easier to remove the film, only rewind one more turn, no more, after feeling the resistance of the end of the film being released from the reel.

Rewinding by Motor Drive MD90 is, of course, much faster and more convenient (see chapter "Motor Drive and Control Functions"). Rewinding by motor leaves the film end protruding from the cassette.

Partially Exposed Films

A partially exposed film should not be rewound completely into the cassette if it is to be reloaded later on. This could be the case if you want to change from a print film to a slide film, say, or from a slower to a faster film. The professional photographer rarely finds himself in the position to do this. He either carries a second camera body loaded with the different type of film, or discards the unexposed length of film. It is usually preferable to waste film rather than time. However, if you need to be economical with your resources, you may proceed as follows:

Note the frame number visible after winding the film following the last exposure. Rewind the film so that the film end still protrudes from the cassette and write the frame number with waterproof felt-tip pen on the film end. The reloading procedure is the same as previously, only remember to put the lens cover on the lens when releasing the shutter between advancing the film from frame to frame, and select a fast shutter speed. Advance the film until the number following that which had been noted on the film end appears in the frame counter and continue shooting.

If, for example, the frame counter showed 18 after the last exposure, you may start shooting after reloading and advancing to frame number 19. This leaves one empty frame between the shooting sequences as a safety measure.

Choosing Your Film

According to information from the photographic trade and industry, only about 5% of 35mm films sold are black-and-white. Of the 35mm colour films sold, under a third are slide films and the majority are colour print films. The proportions differ somewhat from country to country, and SLR camera users tend to use more colour slide film.

Why? On the one hand colour print films produce colour pictures that may be carried around and shown, and they may be used to produce enlargements. So this type of film is useful to the snapshot photographer and to the professional. On the other hand, a slide film produces an image that, provided the photograph is sharp and correctly exposed, produces wonderfully glowing, brilliant colours, producing an image much closer to the original impression. However the effort in projecting it is much greater, and much more equipment is necessary.

The purpose of the photographs will therefore usually be the criterion for the type of film material to select. It is possible to produce prints from a slide, but the quality does not always compare with enlargements produced from negatives. It is also possible to copy negatives to produce slides, but this is not often done. Generally it is preferable to use slide film for the best possible reproduction of an image, and print film for snapshots and personal memories and for large prints.

Black-and-white photography is no longer the cheap alternative to colour pictures. Processing labs often charge more for black-and-white prints than for colour ones. Black-and-white is a medium for expressing special effects, where the monochrome presentation emphasises the statement. It is also used in situations which are limited to black-and-white reproduction, as in the newspaper industry.

Extremely High Speed Film. These are usually rated from ISO 800/30° to 1600/33° and as such are intended mainly for shooting in poor lighting conditions: at night, bad weather, or for sports photography when very fast shutter speeds are essential. They are generally colour films whose speed may be increased by special processing techniques (push processing); in extreme cases even to ISO 3200. However, this is to the detriment of fine grain and brilliant colours.

These very fast films reach the limits of overexposure in normal daylight conditions. Film with speed ISO 1600, used in bright sunlight requiring a shutter speed of $^1/_{1000}$

second and aperture f/16-f/22, leaves very little room for creative manipulation.

High Speed Films. I am talking here about films with speeds ranging from ISO 200/24° to 400/27°. These are films of practically universal application, particularly the ISO 200 ones. For both colour prints and slides this speed offers a good setting range, even in poor lighting conditions, whilst still being useful in bright light. Black-and-white films in this group have a speed of about ISO 400. However, selective focusing with large apertures is no longer possible.

Average Speed films. These are films with speeds from ISO 64/19° to 125/22°. They have great contour sharpness and are very finely grained and as such are particularly suited for large screen slide projection or particularly large prints. At such scales of enlargement their good characteristics may be properly appreciated. The most popular film in these group is the ISO 100/21° which is also the basis for flash guide numbers of flashguns (see chapter "Principles of Flash Photography"). These films are not so universally suitable for interior or dim light photography.

Ultra-Fine-Grain Films. These occupy a special position and offer speeds of between ISO 25/15° to 50/18°. In this class only a few makes and types are offered (e.g. Kodachrome 25, Agfachrome 50, Fujichrome 50) and there are also a few black-and-white films of this type. They are high resolution, finely grained film materials whose excellent qualities can only be appreciated in very large prints and projection of slides to a very large scale. They are less useful for general photography because of their slow speed.

Instant Picture Film. These are in a class of their own

because of their special processing procedures. Using bench top equipment it is possible to process these practically dry and very quickly produce slides. This film, manufactured only by Polaroid produce either colour or black-and-white slides depending on the type and are mainly, but not exclusively, meant for special applications.

Principles of Exposure

During the test run we relied on the program mode for correct exposure. Contrary to what is usually meant by program mode in other cameras, the Minolta 9000 has several programs. Some of these will function automatically and some may be called into operation by the user. The Minolta 9000's program mode is therefore a most versatile aid to the photographer.

Multi-Program Choice

You may know that exposure programs select a combination of aperture and shutter speed to suit the prevailing lighting conditions. The choice lies somewhere between the most suitable aperture value for sufficient depth of field and a fast enough shutter speed to capture moving subjects and to avoid the effects of camera shake. The latter depends on the previously mentioned factors (in the chapter "Short Photographic Guide") of camera support and on the focal length of the lens. The longer focal lengths produce a large image and any movement of the subject or the camera is magnified accordingly.

The Minolta 9000 adjusts automatically to counteract this effect. The normal program mode where setting combinations of aperture f/1.4 at shutter speeds of $^{1}/_{40}$ second are possible, applies only to focal lengths between 35 and 105mm. If a longer focal length lens (from 105mm) is attached, then the camera will

Extreme contrasts make correct exposure very difficult. Integral metering will assess the overall luminance correctly, but the important detail (the person in the top view) is not shown to good effect. Selective metering (spot metering) on the face will produce the correct exposure for the person, the detail through the window will have to suffer as a consequence.

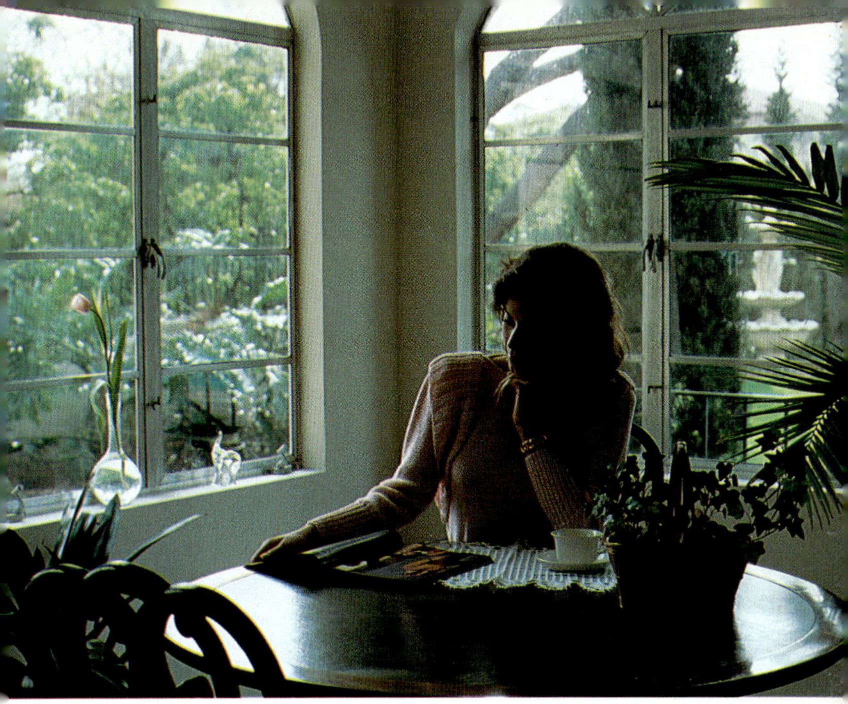

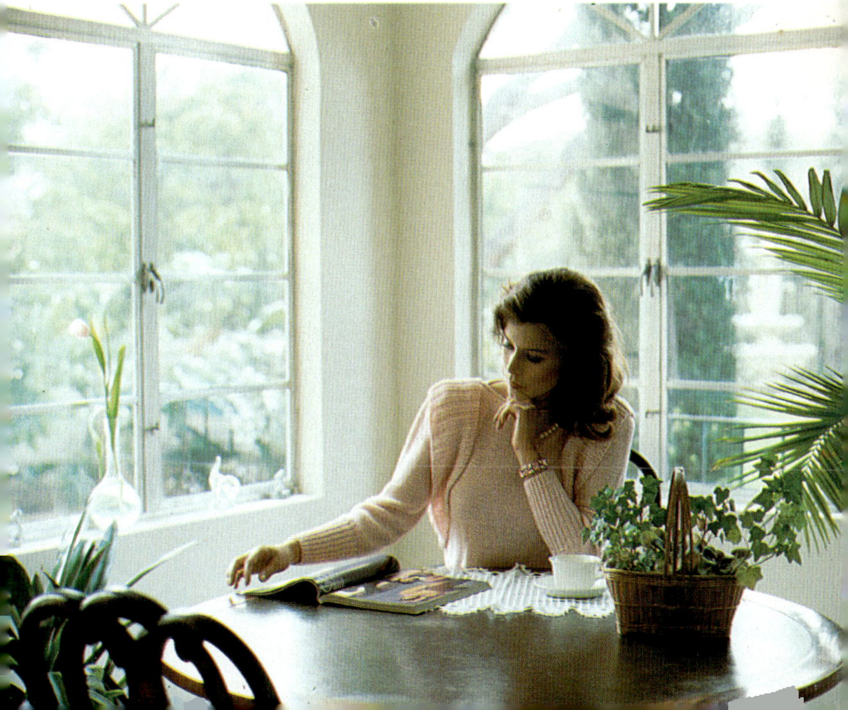

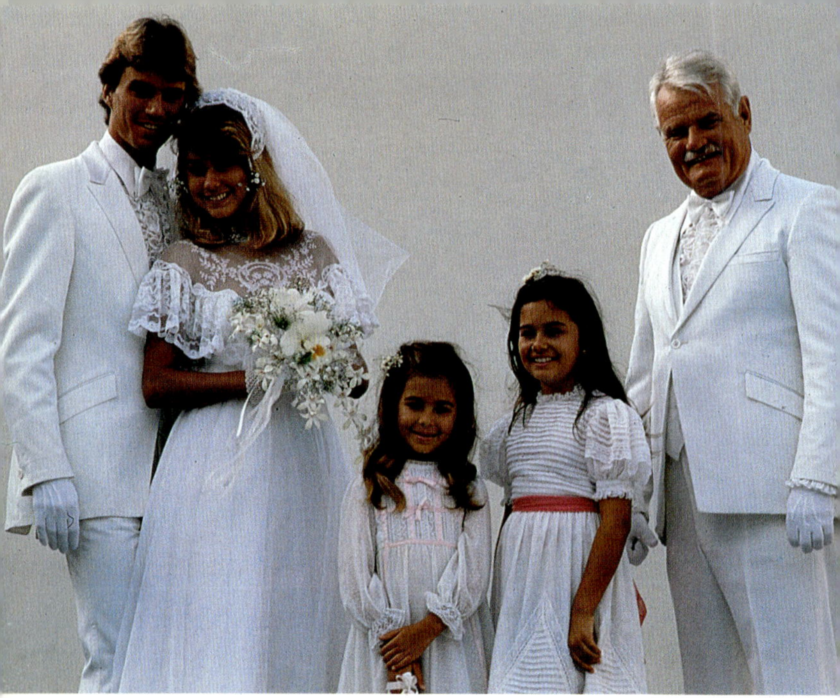

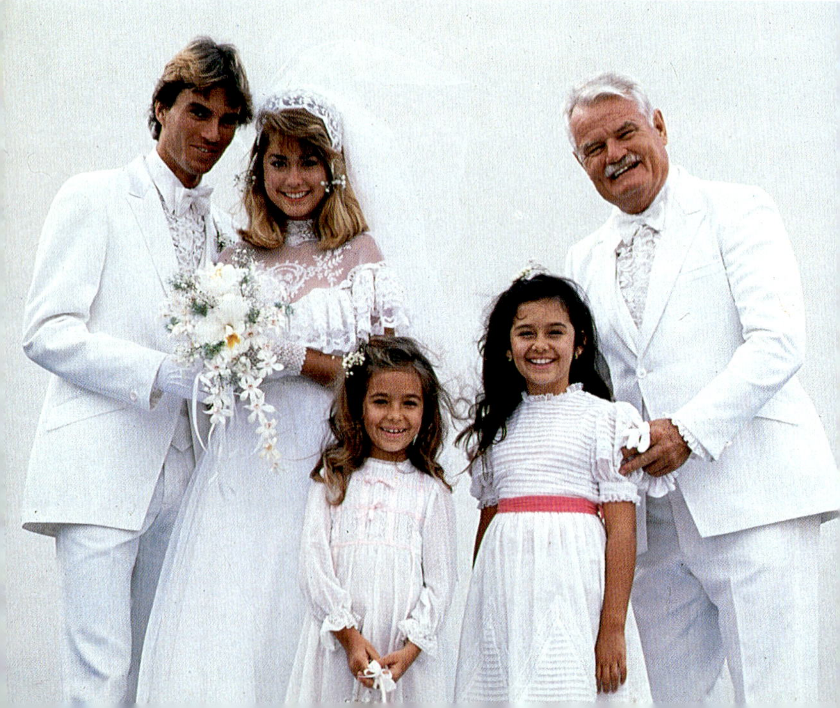

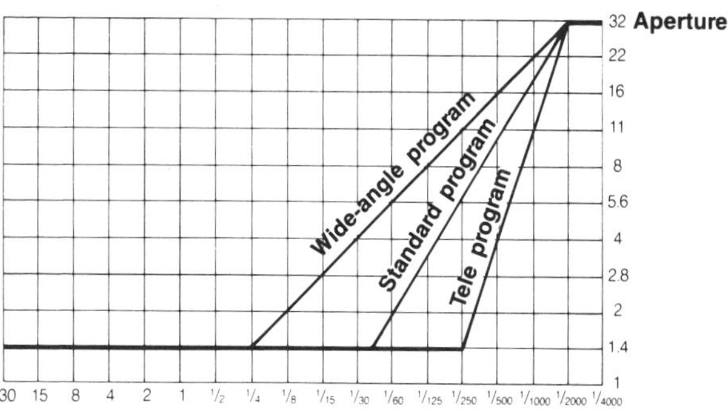

In program mode the camera selects a suitable combination of aperture value and shutter speed to account for the prevailing conditions. The program determines which of the possible combinations shall be applied. The standard program can only select an appropriately slow shutter speed at the largest aperture in poor light. As soon as the shutter speed reduces down to $1/40$ second the aperture begins to decrease as well (rising gradient). In the wide-angle program that is automatically adopted for the shorter focal lengths, stopping down starts with slower shutter speeds, i.e. the program selects as far as possible smaller apertures. The telephoto program prefers fast shutter speeds at the cost of larger apertures, e.g. $1/250$ second at aperture f/1.4

automatically switch to teleprogram. If you refer to the table you can see that the largest aperture starts from a faster shutter speed, so that with a lens speed of f/1.4 the program starts at $1/250$ second (EV9) instead of $1/40$ second (EV 6.5). This means the teleprogram will select a larger aperture and a shorter time for comparable lighting conditions. The standard setting of $1/90$ second and aperture f/2.5 (EV9) corresponds for example in the telephoto program to $1/250$ second and aperture f/1.4. This means a certain insurance against camera shake is built into the teleprogram which also guards against movement blur.

Subjects with predominant light areas will be underexposed if metered by integral metering, because the metering cell will interpret the bright areas as very brightly lit average surfaces and compensate by allowing a smaller dose of light. It will be necessary to overexpose (correct) by two EV stops. Selective metering would also produce the correct exposure.

The wide-angle program for focal lengths between 24 and 28mm functions in the opposite sense. It switches the Minolta 9000 to a wide-angle program where the aperture is already stopped down at shutter speed $1/15$ second (with lens f/2.8). The above mentioned standard setting (EV9) is produced by the combination $1/30$ second and aperture f/4. When using a short focus lens a fast shutter speed is less important as a smaller aperture will produce a reasonable depth of field.

The program is always activated by the lens and the information is electrically conveyed to the camera's electronics. This information is generated by a ROM memory built into every lens. Zoom lenses also supply such information to the camera, even during focal length adjustment. In this way for example, the program will change from wide-angle, to standard, to telephoto program as the setting ring on the 28-135mm zoom lens is moved from the shortest to the longest focal length.

Program Shift

It is not necessary to interfere in the automatic program selection, and it is not possible anyway. If necessary it is possible to adjust the program sequence by using the Program Shift.

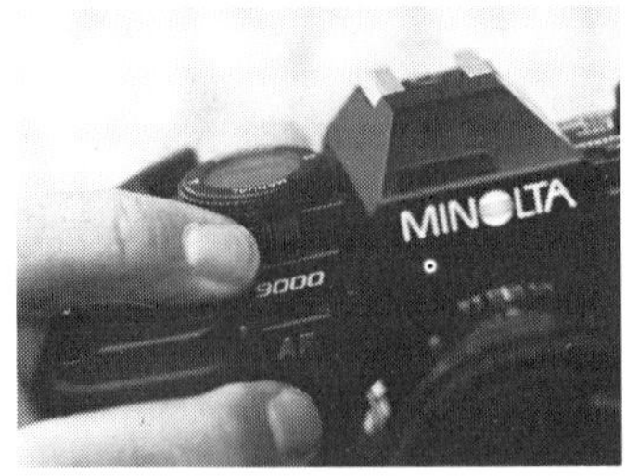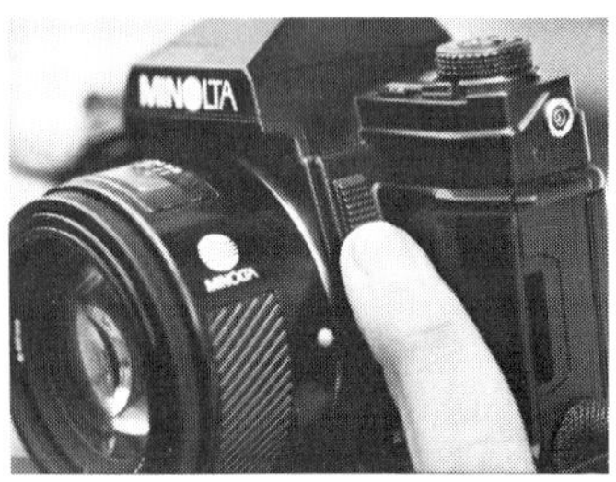

In program shift you operate either the shutter speed key (left) or the aperture key (right). With program shift both keys have the same effect. They have their own function in other program modes.

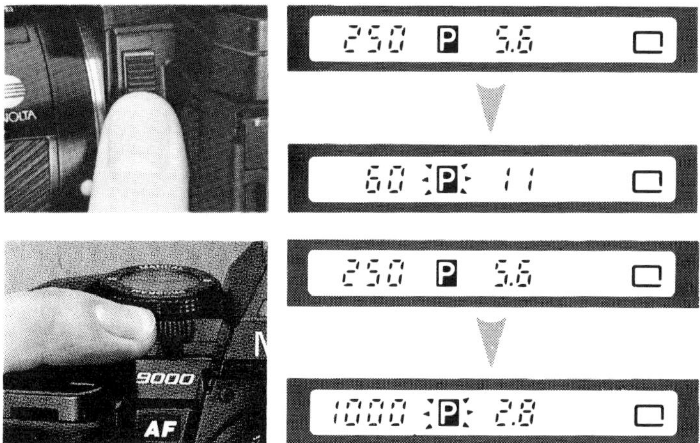

With program shift you can choose a different aperture or shutter speed to those selected by the program mode. If you require a smaller aperture than, say, f/5.6 at shutter speed ¹/₂₅₀ second, then you can select f/11, the shutter speed will be automatically adjusted to ¹/₉₀ second to compensate. The program will then progress according to curve A. Similarly, a shift towards a shorter time of ¹/₁₀₀₀ second will move the curve towards B.

This shift facility is used if you wish to select a different aperture or shutter speed, despite shooting in program mode. The data field and the display bar below the viewfinder image show the combination selected by the program (see "Simple Setting Technique" in the chapter "Short Photographic Guide"). If you now wish to select a shorter time or a smaller aperture, then you simply adjust the value by operating the speed or the aperture key. This can be done by individual pushes or by holding the appropriate key down so that the series of values are displayed in running sequence. In the latter case the program shift moves through the setting range of aperture values for the available lighting conditions, or the fastest or slowest shutter speeds.

The program will take account of changing lighting conditions by a parallel shift of the program sequence. If, for example, the program combination has been shifted by three half stops in the direction of faster shutter speeds and a darker object is presented to the camera, then the exposure time and aperture will be increased. But the time in our example will be in every case the equivalent of one and a half stops less than the combination chosen by the program mode.

Two more remarks about the program shift. Firstly: the program shift remains active only as long as the present metering phase is switched on. As soon as the displays in the viewfinder and the data display disappears the program will return to basic setting. To retain the shift, the finger has to be kept on the release. The fact that a program shift is in operation is indicated by blinking of the "P" in the viewfinder between aperture and shutter speed values. And secondly, and this is hardly of any consequence, the program shift alters only the sequence within a program, and not between wide-angle, standard and telephoto programs.

Aperture Priority Mode

The program modes are ideal for carefree snapping, in particular in combination with the program shift for occasional special adjustments. However, for general individual exposure control the automatic exposure with preselection is better. In this case the aperture or the shutter speed is preselected and the camera's electronics calculate the suitable complementary value. What time or what aperture is selected will depend on the desired sharpness of moving objects or depth of field. This will be described later in the chapter "Principles of Sharpness". In this chapter I would like to cover basic setting principles.

The first preselection facility concerns the aperture. To choose this mode, the function switch is turned until the legend "A" engages against the triangular marker. In the data field a small arrow pointing to the aperture value will appear and in the display bar in the viewfinder the "P" is replaced by "A".

Shown in the display is, as usual, the aperture/shutter speed combination, but this time with a slight difference. Now a change in lighting conditions will only influence the shutter speed. Depending on subject luminance, the shutter speed display will move through the available range within the metering range, and the aperture value will remain constant.

If the shutter speed reaches one of its limit values (30 or 4000), then this value will flash as a signal that the aperture is too small, or too large, for correct exposure. In this case it has to be adjusted, in half stops, similar to program shift. Using a superfast film and f/4 aperture pre-selection, the shutter speed for a sunlit subject would probably be $1/4000$. Push the shutter speed key several times forward, or depress the aperture key until, with decreasing size of aperture, the shutter speed display stops flashing and displays a slower speed. You may then continue taking your pictures.

Shutter Speed Priority Mode

The shutter speed priority mode works in similar fashion. Turn the function switch until "S" (shutter speed) engages next to the triangular marker. The displays are similar to those of the aperture priority mode, only now the arrow in the display field points to the shutter speed and "S" appears next to time value in the viewfinder panel. If the lighting conditions change, then the aperture will show changing values and the shutter speed will remain constant.

When the limit value is reached (e.g. f/1.4 or f/22 with a standard 50mm lens), the aperture value will blink and the time then has to be adjusted accordingly. This should be necessary more often than with aperture pre-selection. The reason being that the aperture range covers only 8 whole (or EV) stops (exposure range about 1:250). The shutter speed range on the other hand covers 17 stops (1:130 000) between the limit values and manages therefore a 500-times larger exposure range without having to adjust the aperture value.

Shutter speed preselection and adjustment is performed similarly to aperture preselection by operating the aperture or the shutter speed key, but in this case the range is covered in full and not in half stops (60, 125, 250, etc.).

The choice of program modes offered by this multi-mode camera, which was offered for the first time by Minolta as early as 1977, makes the choice difficult. What mode should you choose?

Shutter speed priority or S-function is most suitable for sports photography and other moving subjects where movement blur has to be counteracted by fast shutter speeds. This mode, once selected, remains operative even if the lens is changed.

Aperture preselection or A-function keeps the aperture constant and helps to control depth of field. If the lens is changed, this program mode will remain operative only if it is still possible with the type of lens being attached. If you are changing from a standard lens with maximum aperture f/1.4 to a 24mm lens with one of f/2.8, then the camera will adjust the display to f/2.8 and correct the time as well.

In practice the type of program mode selected is not all that crucial. It is possible, both in A-function and in S-function, to change the aperture or the shutter speed, the second value will be adjusted appropriately by electronic control. However, the S- or A-function will determine which value remains constant with changing lighting conditions.

By the way, the exposure values which had been switched to in preselection mode remain in the display even if the camera had been switched off in the meantime. If, for example, the last displayed combination in program mode was $1/125$ second and f/8, then aperture f/8 will be retained if A-function is selected, or shutter speed $1/125$ second, if S-function is chosen. However, if the battery is changed, then the display will return to the basic combination $1/250$ second and f/5.6.

Manual Operation

Finally it is possible to inactivate the Minolta 9000's automatic functions totally and to select the aperture and shutter speed manually. This is useful for individual settings without regard to metered values, with intentional under- or overexposure (but this is also possible with exposure correction - see below), for flash photography with non-system flashguns, such as studio flash, and for long exposures.

To choose this function the shooting mode selector is turned so that MANUAL engages next to the triangular marker. Now two arrows are pointing to the shutter speed and to the aperture values in the data field. In the viewfinder "M" is displayed to the right of the aperture value and to the right of that a correction value, a number between -6.5 and +6.5.

To adjust the shutter speed, move the speed key to the left (shorter time) or to the right (longer time). Each time the key is pushed, the speed changes by one stop (e.g. from $1/125$ to $1/250$ second). To adjust the aperture, the aperture key is moved up (larger aperture), or down (smaller aperture). Again the aperture is changed in half stops. Changing the aperture and shutter speed controls only these values, contrary to the automatic modes. Strictly speaking, this is true also for the automatic mode, but as the aperture and shutter speed values are interlinked in automatic function, adjusting one automatically affects the other.

The light metering function no longer controls the setting values. Nevertheless, it remains active and notifies the photographer whether the combination chosen by him will produce correct exposure. This is indicated by the display of the correction value in the viewfinder to the right of the "M" and the metering value symbol. If the setting is for correct exposure within one quarter aperture stop, then the correction factor displayed will be either +0 or -0 (tending either slightly to "too much" or "too little", as absolute zero is not available).

If the chosen setting is found to be incorrect, then the deviation is indicated in half stops. Therefore +2.5 means an overexposure of 2.5 stops, which may be adjusted by a smaller aperture and/or shorter time. The aperture value has to be adjusted for correction factors of half stops, because the shutter speed is only available in full stops. Similarly if the correction factor was shown as -2 then the aperture could be opened by two whole stops or the aperture by one stop and the time by one stop. If the setting error is more than +6.5 or −6.5 then this value flashes in the display.

Long Exposures

The shutter speeds available on the Minolta 9000 extending down to 30 seconds, cover almost any conceivable subject. This should be sufficient even for dark interior shots but the camera has to be well supported on a tripod or a solid base for such slow speeds. Only if the subject really is very dark and the loaded film is of low speed may it be possible that even longer shutter times are required. But even this is no problem with the Minolta 9000.

If the time key is activated, in manual mode only, beyond the 30 seconds, then the display will indicate "bulb". Depressing the release button in this setting for long exposures will cause the shutter to open and remain open until the pressure on the button is released. Whilst the shutter is open, the word "bulb" is replaced in the display by a seconds count. You can see the seconds being displayed from 0 to 99, or even longer if you have enough patience. This counting is also displayed in the viewfinder, which normally displays nothing during a exposure.

To keep the release depressed for a long time is not really practicable. Even if the camera is supported on a firm tripod, it could still be moved, and who can stand still like a statue anyway? The solution therefore is to release by hand switch and remote control cable RS-1000S or RS-1000L which can be locked in position. (See also "Remote Control" in the chapter "Motor Drive and Control Functions".)

There is no metering display in long exposures. This is because, on the one hand the metering limit is being exceeded, and on the other the one constant value, essential for exposure metering, is no longer constant. This is due to the fact that almost every type of film reacts with reduced speed to long exposures. This loss in film speed, also known as low intensity reciprocity failure, depends on the film and on the subject brightness. It can be compensated for by increasing the exposure time. As a rough rule, the times between 1 second to 10 seconds may be doubled, between 10 seconds and 30 seconds quadrupled, any longer exposures are anyone's guess. Some manufacturers supply precise instructions on long exposure corrections for reciprocity effects.

Light and Exposure

The automatic exposure mode described so far depends in all its variations on metering the subject luminance. This is done automatically, but the user still has considerable scope to influence the process.

Normally the Minolta 9000 measures the subject luminance by so-called centre-weighted integral metering. The metering cell, located at the bottom of the camera, measures the light entering through the lens and being directed, via the partially transparent main mirror and auxiliary mirror. But not all the rays contribute equally to the final measurement. The metering cell reacts more to the rays from the centre section of the frame than to those from the edges. This is because in most pictures that we take the details at the centre of the picture contain the important interest and so the centre-weighted metering corresponds to a correct exposure of the important sections but it is less sensitive to the surrounding light areas (sun, sky) or dark areas (shadows).

The cell measures subject luminance but is unable to assess how this is distributed across the frame. The metering of a subject is generally based on the assumption that the average of the range of brightness distributed across the picture corresponds to an average luminance. This average tone is taken to reflect about 20% of the incident light.

What is surprising about this sweeping assumption is that it produces reasonably exposed pictures in about 90% of situations. Most distributions of luminance usually do correspond to the average and so the Minolta 9000's normal metering method may be relied on.

But what do you do with subjects with unusual tone distribution, such as small, dark figures in a snowscape, or a sunlit figure in front of a dark archway? In both cases the predominant dark or light portions need to be shown in their correct tonal values against the sparsely present average tones. In the case of expansive snowscapes the overall luminance departs a long way from the average. In this case the camera considers the snow as average grey and chooses an exposure to compensate for excessive brightness, i.e. the result will be underexposed. In the second case the large dark area influences the supposed average reading and the result is overexposed.

These are two well-known extreme cases. But there are many instances where predominantly light or dark portions of the subject influence the metering at the cost of the important subject areas. Amongst these for example are portraits taken against the sun or a light sky, night shots in town, sun on water, scenes with a large proportion of sky or extremely bright lights. All these factors could mislead the metering cell and therefore the automatic exposure.

Such misrepresentations are particularly noticeable in slide photography. Not only because a slide film requires exact exposure, but also because the large processing labs usually manage to compensate for exposure errors when enlarging your negatives. The printer does this almost automatically, whether the customer wishes it, or not. This is the reason why some pictures with dominant lightness or darkness often look a lot worse than the negative could produce.

In these special situations it is possible to expose scenes with dominant light areas more generously and those with dominant dark parts, less so. Or one can meter the important detail – the figure within the arched doorway – from close-up so that the doorway no longer influences the metering result.

Spot Metering and Memory Lock

A particularly elegant solution to difficult exposure

In integral metering the metering cell of the Minolta 9000 considers the total light entering the lens.

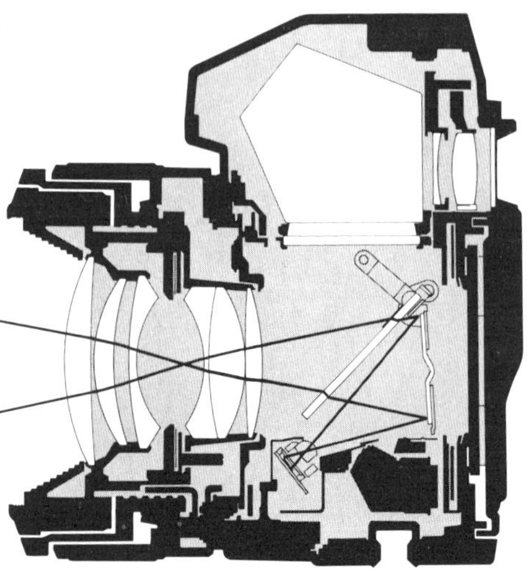

Center-weighted average-metering light path

The metering field is centre weighted. It takes more note of the centre sections which normally show the important detail; the outer zones contribute less to the overall metering result.

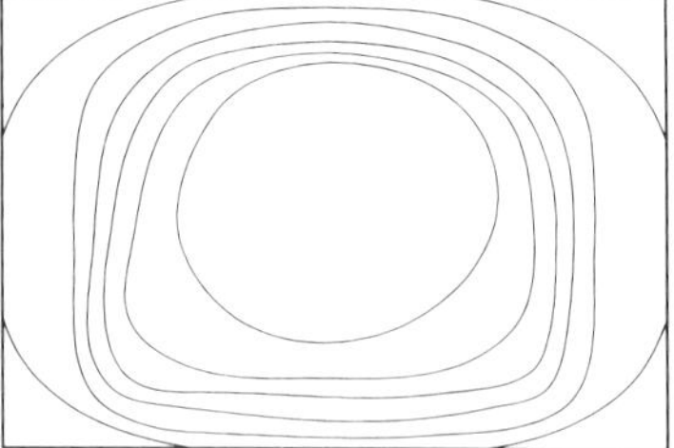

Center-weighted average-metering pattern

problems offered by the Minolta 9000 is the SPOTMETERING facility. In this mode a second cell meters a small beam of light from the first cell, representing just under 3% of the light from the overall frame or, in the case of a 50mm lens, a viewing angle of 6°. This cell also measures in the integral metering process where it contributes to the centre-weighted portion.

Spotmetering is selected via the metering mode selector incorporated in the rewind crank. Turn the knob from AVERAGE to SPOT. A small dot appears within the small rectangle in the viewfinder display bar to indicate

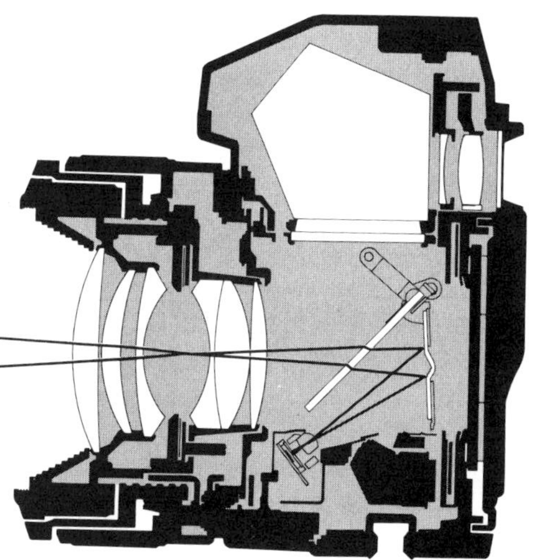

Spot-metering light path

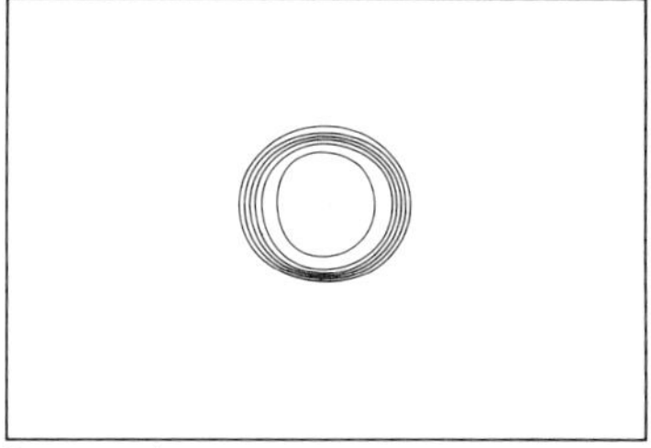

Spot-metering pattern

that this type of metering has been selected.

Using spotmetering mode you may meter small individual areas to disregard the influence of unimportant or undesirable dark or light areas. Provided you choose an area of average tonal value to meter in this way, you can be almost certain that you will obtain perfectly exposed pictures.

In my experience, suitable objects of average tonal value for spotmetering are: grass and lawn in the open air, grey rocks, medium-grey clothing, road surfaces, etc. If you are not sure, try several likely surfaces and choose the most likely out of the group. (In the chapter "Motor

Drive and Control Functions" I describe the databack Super 90 and how such measurements may be stored and averaged out.) Some professional photographers carry an average grey card of 18-20% reflectivity which they position next to the subject and use that as the medium for spot metering. However, this is only feasible if you have sufficient time to arrange your photographic situation.

To obtain an average value it may be simpler to take a reading of a light area, e.g. the sky, or a white, well-lit area, and then one of the darker sections (deep shadow). This is done in manual operation by measuring each area separately and adjusting the exposure until the plus correction and the minus correction factors correspond numerically. The combined result should therefore be the correct one. An example: measuring the light portion at shutter speed 250 ($^1/_{250}$ second) with aperture f/8, the system indicates a correction factor of +1, now measure the dark part and the display shows -4. Now adjust the speed to 125. The correction reading would be +2 and -3. Now the aperture may be adjusted to f/5.6 and the correction factors should be +2.5 and -2.5. The final exposure is therefore $^1/_{125}$ at f/5.6.

The correction factors can only be displayed in half stops and the average value may sometimes not be

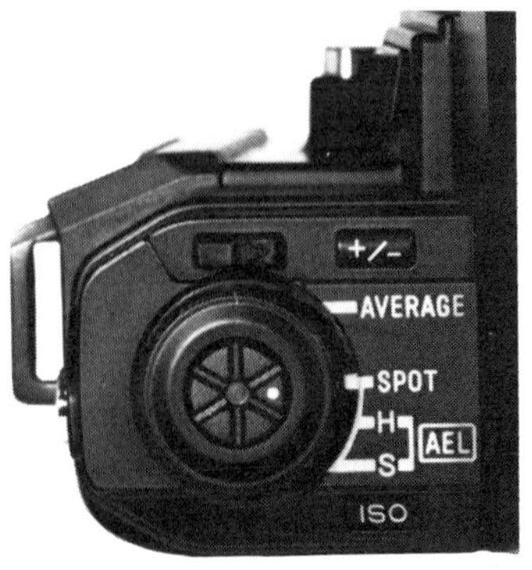

The metering types are selected by this switch: AVERAGE (centre weighted integral metering) or SPOT (selective metering). The other settings H and S shift the assessment of the data (for light and shade), they have no effect on what area is metered.

exactly in the middle; for example +2.5 and -3. The remaining difference is only a quarter stop and should not really matter.

The metering point suitable for spot metering only rarely lies at the centre of the picture. The measured result may therefore be stored in a program mode (P, A or S) after metering and before the shot is actually taken, to allow selection of the required frame. The small grey memory button marked AEL (Auto Exposure Lock) is used for this purpose. Point the camera to meter the measuring spot, press the memory button and keep it pressed, move the camera to obtain the required frame and release. The measured result remains in memory as long as the memory button is kept depressed. As soon as you release the shutter the Minolta 9000 will take a new measurement. Memory lock may also be used in integral metering, although in this metering mode it is very rarely needed.

Measuring Highlights and Shadows

It is not always possible to find a surface with good average tonal values, as for example with the previously mentioned snowscape. But we may assume that the almost 100% reflecting snow-covered surface has five times the reflectivity of the 20% average tone. If we now meter the snow-covered surface and increase the exposure $\times 5$ (ca $2^{1}/_{2}$ EV or lens stops), then we should obtain the same result as would have been achieved by average surface metering. The Minolta 9000 helps you by integrated auto correction. To make use of this facility you turn the metering mode selector from SPOT to H (Highlight = metering of light tones). If you now depress the AEL button during metering, the camera will automatically correct the exposure by 2.5 EV; for example from $^{1}/_{125}$ second to $^{1}/_{20}$ second. What is adjusted depends on the function mode: in P- and in A-modes it will be the time, in S-mode the aperture, and in manual operation the +/- display.

Turning the measuring type selector to S (metering of shadows) the procedure is similar, but in the opposite direction. In this case the important detail in the picture is measured, i.e. the part which is to show detail, not an empty black area. Depressing the AEL button during metering will cause the automatic correction function to shift the exposure by 2.5 EV, e.g. from $^1/_{15}$ second to $^1/_{90}$ second and compensate for the excessively long exposure that would otherwise be used for the predominantly dark object.

Exposure Correction

Less exact but quicker than spotmetering is exposure correction by the correction key +/- which is located at the top next to the metering mode selector. Depress the correction key: the symbol "+/-" appears below the cross bar in a small rectangle in the data field of the function selector and to the right of "0.0". If the shutter speed key is now pushed to the left, in the direction of the prism housing, while keeping the correction key depressed, the display increases in half EV values (0.5, 1.0, 1.5 up to 4.0) and in the rectangle only the + remains visible. In the viewfinder the reading will be 0.0 and +/- (otherwise nothing) and this will also count to +0.4. As soon as the correction key is released, the corrected value of shutter speed and aperture appears in the data field, together with the + symbol in the rectangle. In the viewfinder, next to the exposure display, the correction value flashes (e.g. +1).

The AF f/4.5-5.6, 75-300mm zoom lens is ideal for animal photography. It is invaluable on photographic safari where automatic focusing and exposure modes keep step with continuously changing situations.
Photo: Joachim F. Richter

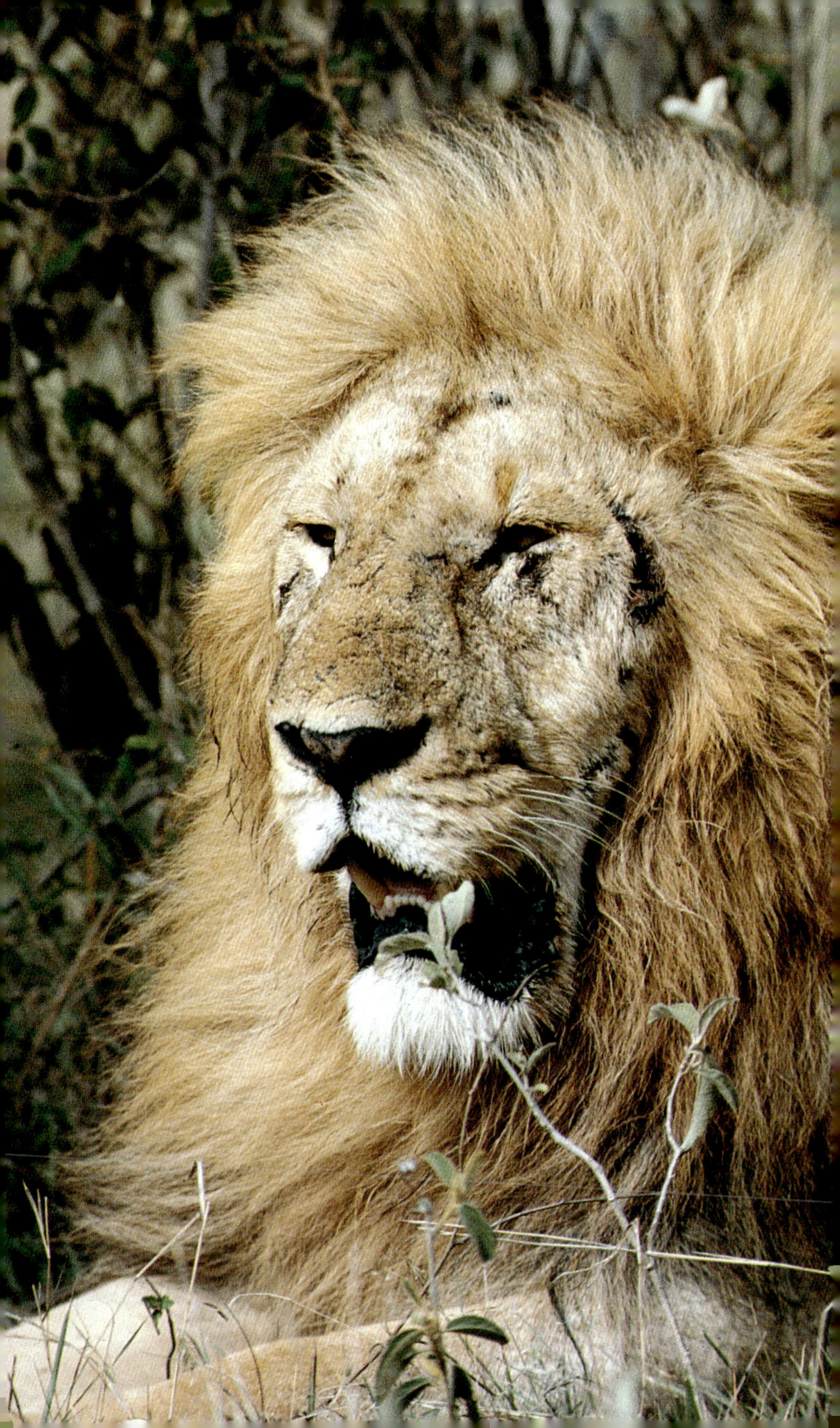

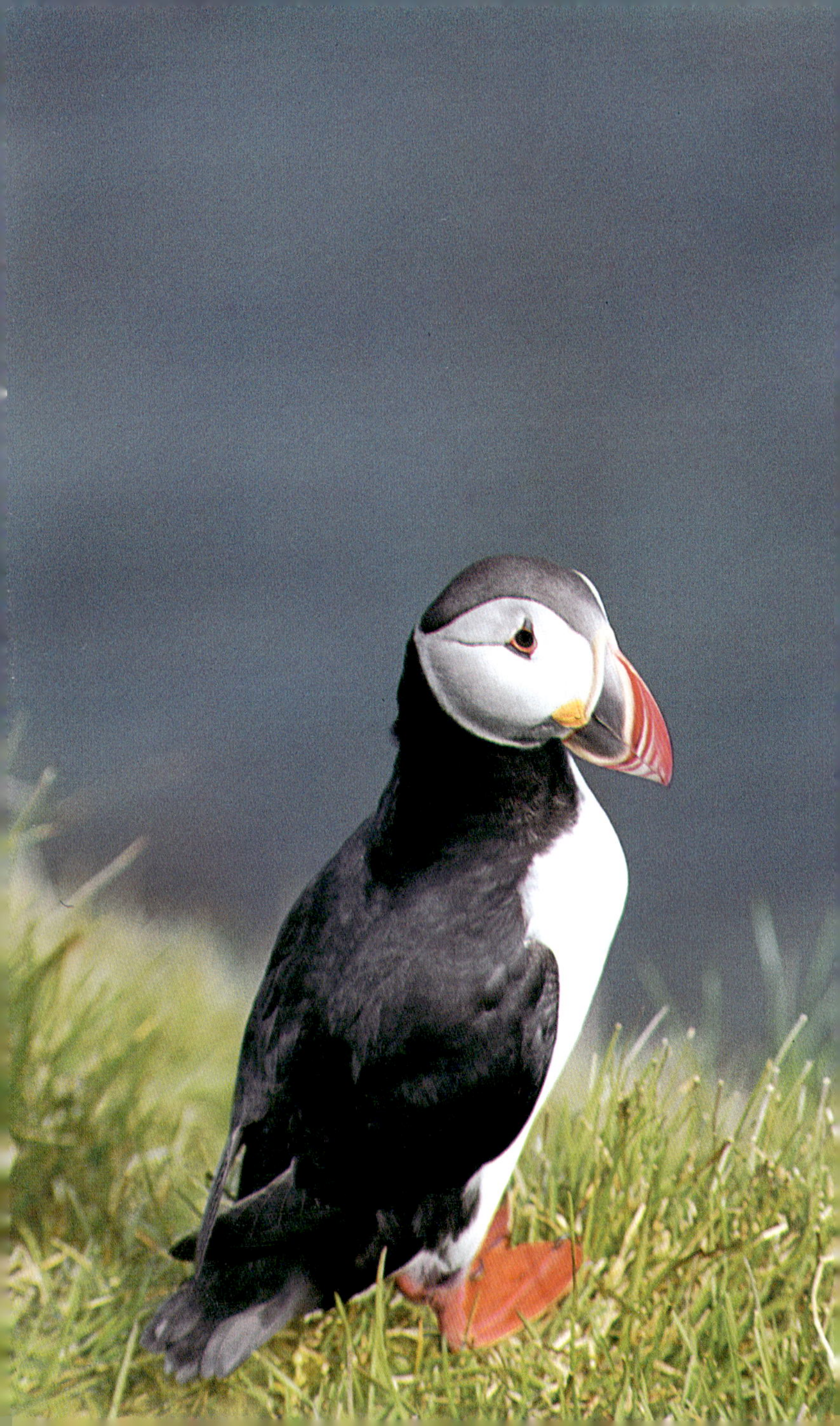

In the above case the correction is an intentional overexposure. If the shutter speed key is moved to the right, then the displayed values will be minus values, i.e. intentional underexposure, or any selected plus-correction is reduced. The exposure correction can only be used together with the shutter speed key. The aperture key can select different aperture/shutter speed combinations, as described previously, but it cannot effect correction in this mode.

This method is preferable for a whole series of shots, all of which need to be taken with the same correction factor. This saves having to perform new spot metering for every frame. A plus correction amends the exposure for dark objects in front of light backgrounds, e.g. the portrait against the light sky, and a minus correction covers the opposite situation, the figure in front of a dark archway. By how much you have to correct is a matter of experience. As a general guideline I would choose about $+1^1/_2$ or $-1^1/_2$ stops respectively. If the background covers a rather large area, compared with the main subject, or if the contrast is extreme, then you may need an even bigger correction factor.

Exposure correction can also be used to achieve special effects by intentional underexposure, or to obtain delicate, transparent colours by overexposure.

The exposure correction plays a special role in manual operation. In this mode it does not change the aperture or shutter speed setting, because this is now only possible by operating the shutter speed and aperture keys. However, it changes the viewfinder display of the required adjustment for correct exposure. Let's say the setting is $^1/_{125}$ second and f/8 and the viewfinder

---

The animal photographer is greatly assisted by certain accessories such as the 5m long remote release cable RS-1000SL, or the infra-red remote release IR-1N. A well hidden and camouflaged camera, controlled from a safe distance, will allow large reproduction scales even of very shy animals. *Photo: Joachim F. Richter*

indicates −1.5, i.e. an underexposure of $1^1/_2$ stops, then this may be corrected by adjusting the shutter speed, or aperture, or a combination of the two. If you performed the correction to, say 125 and f/4.5 then the "correct" signal will appear, namely +0 or −0. But it is also possible to enter a correction factor of, say, −1.5 by depressing the +/- key and operating the shutter speed key; the viewfinder display indicates in that case correct exposure at 125 and f/8. This procedure corresponds to an instruction to the computer of "I wish to achieve an underexposure of $1^1/_2$ stops with this setting" and the computer confirms "all right, in this case the exposure is correct".

Lastly there is the possibility to correct the circumstances of the subject being photographed; i.e. to lighten shadow areas. To do this we generally employ flash, as described in the chapter "Principles of Flash Photography". Again the Minolta 9000 offers sophisticated solutions to this problem.

Metering and Setting Limits

The metering range of the Minolta 9000 is subject to limits. Minolta themselves state the lower metering limit as EV1 and the upper limit as EV20. This refers to a lens with lens speed f/1.4 and film ISO setting 100, furthermore, it applies to all shooting modes. The luminance limits are between 0.25 and about 130 000 cd/m² (i.e.: nits).

Applying this to exposure values we find that the lower limit lies at 1 second and aperture f/1.4. The metering mode indicator in the viewfinder (rectangle on the right, with or without dot) begins to blink as soon as the time becomes longer at the largest aperture. In poorer lighting conditions still, even slower shutter speeds could be displayed in the viewfinder, but these are no longer reliable.

The flashing metering mode indicator therefore has to be interpreted as a warning. The exposure may no longer be correct. The further you exceed the limit, the greater the metering uncertainty. In addition it has to be considered that film characteristics add further to this problem, (see section "Long Exposures"). But as this luminance of 0.25 cd/m^2 corresponds say to a very dark corner of a room, it usually presents no real problem.

In the case of spotmetering, this lower limit is shifted upwards by 2 to $2^1/_2$ stops because the light is measured by only one of the cells, which makes the system less sensitive. Under very dim conditions this may be counteracted by highlight metering (see previous chapter): meter the brightest part of the subject and correct by AEL memory lock to average exposure.

The upper metering limit need concern us even less. It corresponds to about ten times the luminance of a sunlit daylight scene! Usually the setting limit (see below) is reached long before that.

The luminance limits are absolute values, but the required exposure depends on film speed. Consequently the lower limit display will already start to blink for shorter times for the higher ISO settings (in the case of ISO 1600 at about $^1/_{15}$ second) and for lower ISO values not until slower speeds are displayed (ISO 25 starting at 8 second).

The metering limit should not be confused with the setting limit. The latter depends on the limit values of the shutter (30 seconds and $^1/_{4000}$ second) or that of the lens attached at a particular time (e.g. f/4 and f/22 for the 35-70mm zoom lens). In this case these limit values will flash in the viewfinder.

If you are shooting in aperture priority mode with a film speed setting of ISO 1600 and an aperture of f/1.4, measuring, as described, a bright landscape, then the shutter speed will almost certainly be insufficient, i.e. the 4000 will flash. Similarly in S-mode (shutter speed priority) flashing of the aperture value (and in PROGRAM mode flashing of shutter speed and aperture) means that the setting limits have been reached.

If the slowest shutter speed and largest aperture are selected (30 seconds and f/1.4), then the measuring limit could coincide with the setting limit. In that case the aperture value, the shutter speed value and the metering type symbol will all light up.

Viewfinder Illumination

In order to render the viewfinder display visible, even under poor lighting conditions, the Minolta 9000 is equipped with viewfinder illumination. As soon as the luminance of the subject drops below 60 cd/m^2 a series of lamps automatically light up in the viewfinder. These lamps are visible from the top through the illumination window in the prism housing. It is therefore possible to read the exposure data even in complete darkness, but not that on top of the camera. As soon as the ambient lighting conditions improve the lamps go out immediately, and they also go out whenever the viewfinder display disappears. They do not light up when the film is loaded before it is advanced to the first frame.

Eyepiece Cover for Stray Light

The metering cells in the camera not only react to the light entering through the lens, but also to any light entering from the top through the eyepiece, passing through the mirror and falling onto the metering cell. Normally this path is sufficiently obscured by the eye being pressed against the eyepiece when the amount of light able to pass through is negligible compared with that which enters through the lens. The situation is different, however, if the camera is supported on a tripod and you are not looking through the eyepiece when taking the photograph, i.e. during self-timer shots, remote control shots, etc. The remedy is simple in such cases: you close the eyepiece cover. This is the small black lever to the right of the eyepiece which is rotated clockwise so that the red blade becomes visible in the eyepiece. The information reaching the cell is now correct.

Multiple Exposures

The usual practice of coupling the film transport to the shutter wind prevents more than one exposure being madeon one frame and also saves film from being wasted by moving the transport too far on. However, it is possible to disengage this coupling for intentional double or multiple exposures. To effect this you push the disconnection key to the left and hold it there during the initial movement of the transport lever. The disconnection key is the little grey key on the right top of the camera back panel to the right of the AEL key; it need not be held for the entire movement of the wind-on lever.

The wind-on lever now will only cock the shutter without moving the film by even a millimetre or advancing the frame counter. The second exposure will be made exactly coinciding with the first. For any more exposures on the same frame the whole procedure is repeated.

The multiple exposures act cumulatively on the film. The exposure value for a normal double exposure should therefore be halved (best by an exposure correction of −1). But if you are making multiple exposures on a dark background, for instance in the study of movement, perhaps with flash, and if it does not illuminate the background as well, then it is better to use the normal exposure value. The same applies also to trick photographs with masked lens.

Principles of Sharpness

As mentioned previously, the Minolta 9000's automatic focusing facility is based on an assessment of sharpness of an image projected by the lens. Because of this direct assessment of the image, this AF function is different from the distance metering of compact miniature cameras and other SLR makes and as such does not depend on the image distance (down to macro range) or on the focal length of the lens.

Minolta's Measuring Principles

First a little technology. The ray of light directed into the camera base for sharpness metering (see also chapter "Controls and Functions") is projected onto a sensor system situated at an equivalent plane. An arrangement of micro lenses and photocells split the projected image into partial images created by opposite lens edges. This method corresponds to the split image focusing screen generally used in SLR cameras. If the image is in sharp focus the partial images coincide exactly. But if the image is either in front of or behind the focusing plane, then the partial images will be shifted with respect to each other.

The sensors analyse the brightness distribution of the projected partial images and ascertain from this information the exact lateral position or displacement. In case of congruent partial images the detail brightnesses are in phase, but if the images are incongruent, the brightnesses are out of phase.

These two conditions may be recognized by different output signals of the sensor system and supply on the one hand the sharp/unsharp signal and on the other, in case of unsharpness, the directional signal as an indication of whether the optimum plane of sharpness lies in front of or behind the sensor plane.

The "unsharp" signal activates the motor, the directional signal determines the direction of rotation. The focusing motor switches off as soon as the signals are in phase: this means the lens is set for optimum sharpness. The lens stays in this position of optimum focusing sharpness. There is another control function which brakes the motor shortly before it reaches the desired setting so that the AF function overshoots the optimum focusing point as little as possible and the motor has to reverse only occasionally.

How Effective Is the Focusing Facility?

There are some common criteria between visual and electronic recognition of image sharpness: both require at least brightness and contrast of the details that have to be brought into sharp focus. Minolta state as the working range EV2 to EV19 at ISO 100. This means in practical terms that the lower limit lies at about 0.5 cd/m^2 luminance. The upper limit lies far above any normally occurring subject luminance. The limiting value (= exposure at 1/2 second at f/1.4) is therefore only 1 EV higher than the lower limit of exposure metering. Furthermore, this metering limit also presupposes sufficient image contrast. Even with the best intentions and good lighting you cannot expect the Minolta 9000 to bring into sharp focus a featureless, uniformly white wall. Even so, the least measurable detail contrast depends also on the available light: in good light the camera will be able to cope with less contrast than in poor light. The exact definition of limit points is not important as the camera will inform you anyway by illumination of the two red arrow points when and if it is unable to cope with automatic focusing.

These circumstances are similar to those of our own

visual abilities. The camera sees about as sharply as the human eye with 20/20 vision, no better and no worse. The focusing precision corresponds also to our visual focusing ability. However, the camera's performance is consistent, whilst many camera users are not always capable of seeing and focusing sharply. Either out of ignorance or vanity many do not wear glasses who should do so. And finally the depth of field often bridges any small errors in focusing except when very large apertures are used.

Fast Reaction

The first mirror reflex cameras with autofocus reacted rather slowly, or had only an electronic sharpness control consisting of manual setting and signals (LEDs and/or bleep tones) indicating when focusing was correct. This was found to be too cumbersome. Only after the fast focusing AF reflex cameras were introduced, above all the Minolta 7000, could the market be convinced of its worth. After all, the experienced photographer can focus just as well as the camera's electronics, but he is not as fast. If you have to fumble half a minute on the setting ring to obtain optimum focusing; then you will find the half second that it takes the Minolta's AF mechanism to achieve best results no time at all. The most important feature for the professional is not just the precision of the camera's focusing ability, but its fast reaction.

Another important factor is that the sharpness setting will change with a moving subject, particularly with the Minolta 9000. I have mentioned previously (see "Test Run" in the chapter "Short Photographic Guide") that the camera will automatically follow a moving subject as long as it is kept within the target rectangle in the viewfinder and the finger is kept on the release button. The focusing setting is stored only after a slightly stronger pressure on the release button and this is indicated by illumination of the green circular diode. The acoustic test signal, if activated, also confirms that the focusing setting has been stored. This is the point when you should release the shutter because the subject may move closer or farther away, but the focusing setting will remain as it was, unless, of course, the release button is released altogether and newly activated.

The automatic focusing facility works fast, but not as fast as a flash. The focusing motor moves towards the point of optimum sharpness in subsequent phases of reduced speed to avoid overshooting the focusing point. If we now take a moving object it may be the case that the motor is always just that little bit behind without actually catching up. The remedy is to get the better of the programmed procedure: if the object approaches the camera you start by focusing on something close to the camera, e.g. the floor, then focus on the moving object to release immediately, as soon as the green light illuminates. If the object moves away from the camera then you focus first on infinity before following the object. This pre-setting procedure is quite quick and effective.

Using a motor drive you can couple it to the release and focusing facility so that is will release only if correct focusing is attained (see chapter "Motor Drive and Control Functions").

Focus Lock

The important object to be represented in sharp focus may not always lie within the 1.2x2.5mm target rectangle which is even smaller than the spot metering field. Similarly to exposure metering, first you have to measure the important object and then store the measured result. Depress release lightly until the bleep-tone notifies storage of focusing setting then the desired framing may be selected. The release has to be held depressed up to the moment the shot is taken, otherwise the sharpness setting will be lost.

This focus lock facility is useful also in situations where the subject cannot be properly metered perhaps because it is too dark or lacking in contrast. In this case you focus on a suitable object at the same distance and keep this setting in memory. In poor lighting conditions the entire scene is usually too dark. In that case the only remedy would be an illuminated object such as a torch or handlamp.

For interior shots with AF flashguns (4000, 2800 or 1800) the AF metering flash will provide the correct focusing information (refer to "Light for AF" in the chapter "Using Flash"). The metering flash activates only when the release is depressed and the setting is also stored at the same time.

Sharpness in the Viewfinder

Regardless of the automatic focusing facility the image in the viewfinder should also be sharp. The Minolta 9000's viewfinder eyepiece may be adjusted to suit individual vision. To adjust it turn the setting button next to the eyepiece until the target rectangle in the centre of the viewfinder appears sharpest pointing the camera at a bright surface, e.g. the sky.

The range of this continuous setting facility corresponds to dioptre values of +1 to −3, i.e. moderate long-sightedness to average short-sightedness. If you need stronger correction values then you may attach additional correction lenses EC 1000 available from −4 to + 3 dioptres. In my own particular case of −4 dioptres I manage nicely with an additional lens of −2 dioptres (combined setting range −1 to −5 dioptres). In theory it is possible to correct sights within −7 to +4 dioptres, because the correction lenses EC 1000 were originally intended for the Minolta 7000 which has no integrated correction lens.

For those of you with normal vision the eyepiece setting would be at about −1, at about the centre position of the setting range. The viewfinder image appears at an apparent distance of 1m. The eyepiece setting affects the rectangular and circular areas at the centre of the viewfinder, but not the LCD below, which appear to be a little closer. One problem for those of you who are wearing glasses is the question of whether you should view with or without glasses, especially those with short sight. If the sight is corrected for viewing without glasses, then you have to take your glasses off when viewing through the eyepiece and put them on again when looking directly at the subject. If you decide to view with glasses, then you cannot see the entire viewfinder image without having to strain your eyes to see the edges, and in particular the display bar. Which is the lesser of these two evils? That must be a matter of individual preference. Severely short-sighted users may find it easier to view with glasses. In any case I would try out both possibilities and then decide on the preferable solution.

Interchangeable Focusing Screens

You will probably choose manual focusing only on rare occasions, because the autofocusing facility works well. The normal all-matt screen is therefore ideal. If necessary it is possible to focus manually, and the AF target rectangle and the spot metering circle present no obstacles to image assessment. The focusing screen may be exchanged from a range of varieties for special applications.

To change the focusing screen is not as difficult as it may seem. The viewfinder housing is an integral part of the camera; the screen therefore has to be inserted through the lens opening. First, the lens is detached and the camera is put on a flat surface, with the opening facing you. Interchangeable focusing screens are supplied in plastic containers. Put the open container next to the camera and hold it, and a pair of tweezers, at the ready.

Carefully pull out the retaining spring located on top in the lens flange immediately below the contact strip. The screen frame together with the focusing screen will fold up and down onto the mirror. Using the tweezers at all times, grasp the screen by its tag (left of centre), lift it carefully out of the camera and deposit it vertically in the screen container next to the exchange screen. Now grasp the new screen by its tag with the tweezers, insert it carefully through the lens flange into the camera and position it on the screen frame so that the tag of the screen comes to rest on the broad tag a little to the right of the frame. The screen has to be straight on the frame, use the tweezers to straighten it if necessary.

Now stand the camera on its head, the screen and the frame folded back against the screen bed at the top of the viewfinder. If necessary you can help the frame along with the tweezers. Then press the screen frame against the black tag – again only with the tweezers – until it engages. The new screen is now installed. The removed screen can be safely stored flat in the empty compartment of the plastic container.

It is important only to perform all these manipulations with tweezers. Never touch the screen, and particularly the mirror, with your fingers! This would leave fingermarks which, although invisible in the photograph, would be irritating in the viewfinder. The retaining spring in the viewfinder also should only be handled with the tweezers. Never put your hand inside the Minolta 9000!

Assortment of Screens

Altogether there are five replacement screens available for the Minolta 9000:

○ **Screen G** (= general) this is the screen that is supplied with the camera, a microprism type all-matt screen with Fresnel surface and the previously-mentioned AF target rectangle measuring 1.25x2.5mm and spot metering circle of 5.5mm diameter. The Fresnel structure is a very fine ringed pattern (at 0.04mm intervals) which is normally not visible. The Fresnel pattern concentrates the light distribution of the focusing screen optimally on the viewfinder eyepiece and thus ensures uniform illumination of the entire viewfinder image, covering the edges and into the corners.

○ **Screen L** (= line grid) is similar to the above screen G, but has only a 6mm line grid to facilitate exact horizontal and/or vertical adjustment of the subject. Screen L is therefore particularly well suited for architectural photographs, reproductions, etc. But it may also be used for general photography. I find the line grid useful for all kinds of situations; some photographers, on the other hand, think it a nuisance.

○ **Screen S** (= scale) is also similar to screen G, but has a reticule with millimeter graduations. This is particularly useful in macrophotography to assess the reproduction ratio (see "Macro Lenses" in the chapter "All about Lenses").

○ **Screen C** (= clear) is a clear focusing screen, i.e. without a matt surface but with the same target and measuring areas. On this screen the viewfinder image appears particularly bright which is useful for poor lighting, night photography, etc., but it cannot be used for manual focusing because of the absence of the matt surface.

○ **Screen PM** unlike the above screens this has no target and no metering area. Instead it has a conventional split-image indicator and a microprism ring for easy manual focusing (see "Manual Focusing Aids"). The outer microprism ring corresponds to the spot metering circle and the AF target field may be assumed to correspond to the split image screen in

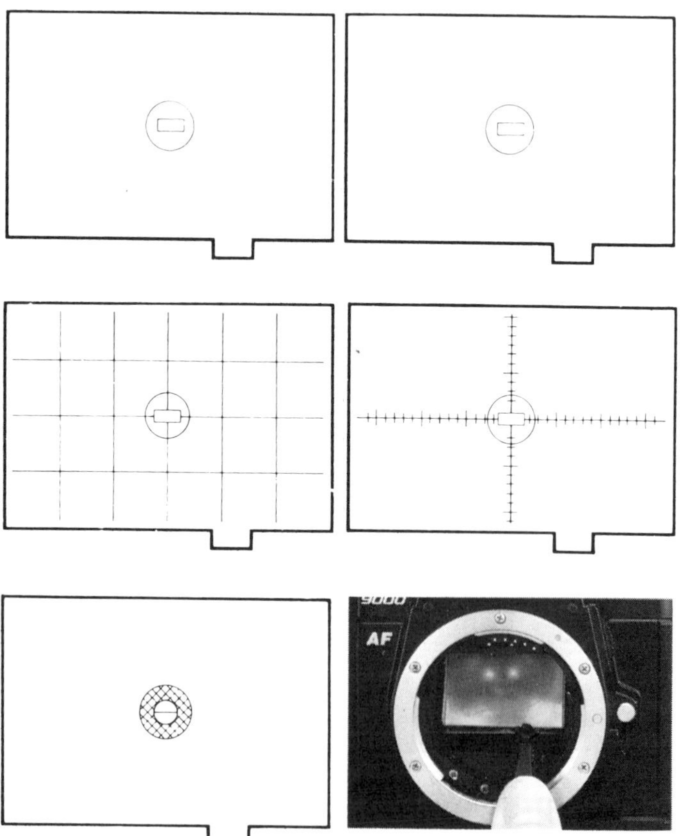

Changing the focusing screen on your Minolta 9000 adapts it for very specialised tasks. Top left: Type G. Top right: Type C. Centre left: Type L. Centre right: Type S. Bottom left: Type PM. Bottom right: Inserting a screen with tweezers.

the centre of the metering circle. Screen PM is useful if you often come across situations where the automatic focusing has difficulties.

By the way, Screen PM is identical to the Screen PM which is supplied for the Minolta 7000. In principle all the other screens used for the Minolta 7000 can be used in the 9000 (Types G, L and S); however these have no spot metering circle because it is a facility which is not offered with the 7000.

Interchangeable focusing screens have been provided to allow the camera to be adapted to special applications. It was not the intention to constantly change them, the procedure would be too cumbersome.

Manual Focusing Aids

If the AF facility fails, then the conditions for visual focusing are usually also difficult. The normal focusing aids generally provided in conventional SLR cameras, such as split-image indicator and microprism ring in the focusing screen, are useful aids that are desirable as backup. One such aid is the focusing screen PM.

The split-image aid consists of two wedge-shaped sections incorporated in a screen. By their optical construction they split an image that is not properly focused along a horizontal section, shifting the two image halves against each other within the 2.5mm diameter circle.

The microprism ring with outer diameter 5.5mm surrounds the split image screen. An unsharp image has a characteristic shimmering appearance that disappears as soon as the image is brought into sharp focus. This is brought about by a pattern of tiny wedged surfaces, similar to the split image screen at the centre. These too split the image into lots of small partial elements. The wedged surfaces are the sides of the tiny 0.16mm rectangular prisms – the microprisms. The ring contains 750 of these.

These two focusing aids complement each other for the best possible manual focusing in different situations. The split image indicator allows quick focusing because the eye reacts more easily to the greater or lesser shifting of partial images, than to increasing or decreasing sharpness. This applies in particular to focusing in poor light. However, it is important to find subject lines that run more or less vertically to the cross-section of the split image in order to be able to assess their alignment or appropriate facial lines or horizontal lines for shots in vertical format. This condition corresponds to detail selection for focusing in auto focus mode, because the measured phase shift of the AF sensors tests also for horizontal misalignment.

In the microprism ring the multiple image splitting causes a ragged dismemberment of the image detail that produces abrupt sharpness by its sudden disappearance when optimum focusing is achieved. This transition is not dependent on direction, and the microprism ring is therefore suitable for manual focusing on fine structures where a split image indicator, and often the autofocus also, would be quite useless. The focusing is particularly precise because the fine structure shimmers for a slight deviation from the optimum setting if the camera is moved slightly.

Both focusing aids, the microprism ring and the split image indicator work only for aperture openings down to about f/5.6. In practical application this only has any effect in the extreme macro range (as soon as there are

---

The picture perspective depends only on the camera position. But as the wide-angle lens covers a wide viewing angle and the depth of field is large for small apertures it is possible to achieve a particularly impressive spatial effect with this combination.   Photo: Jürgen Lehr

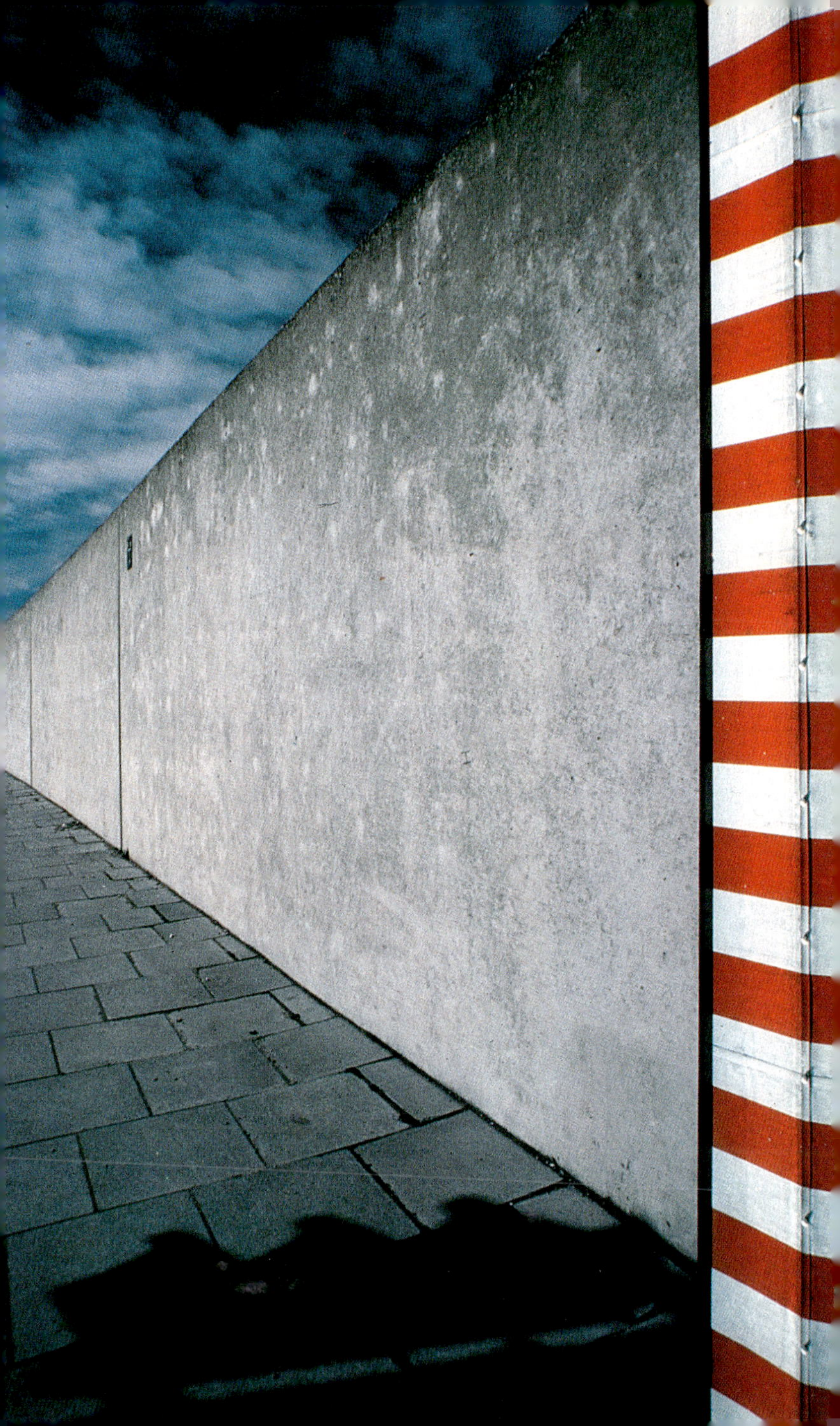

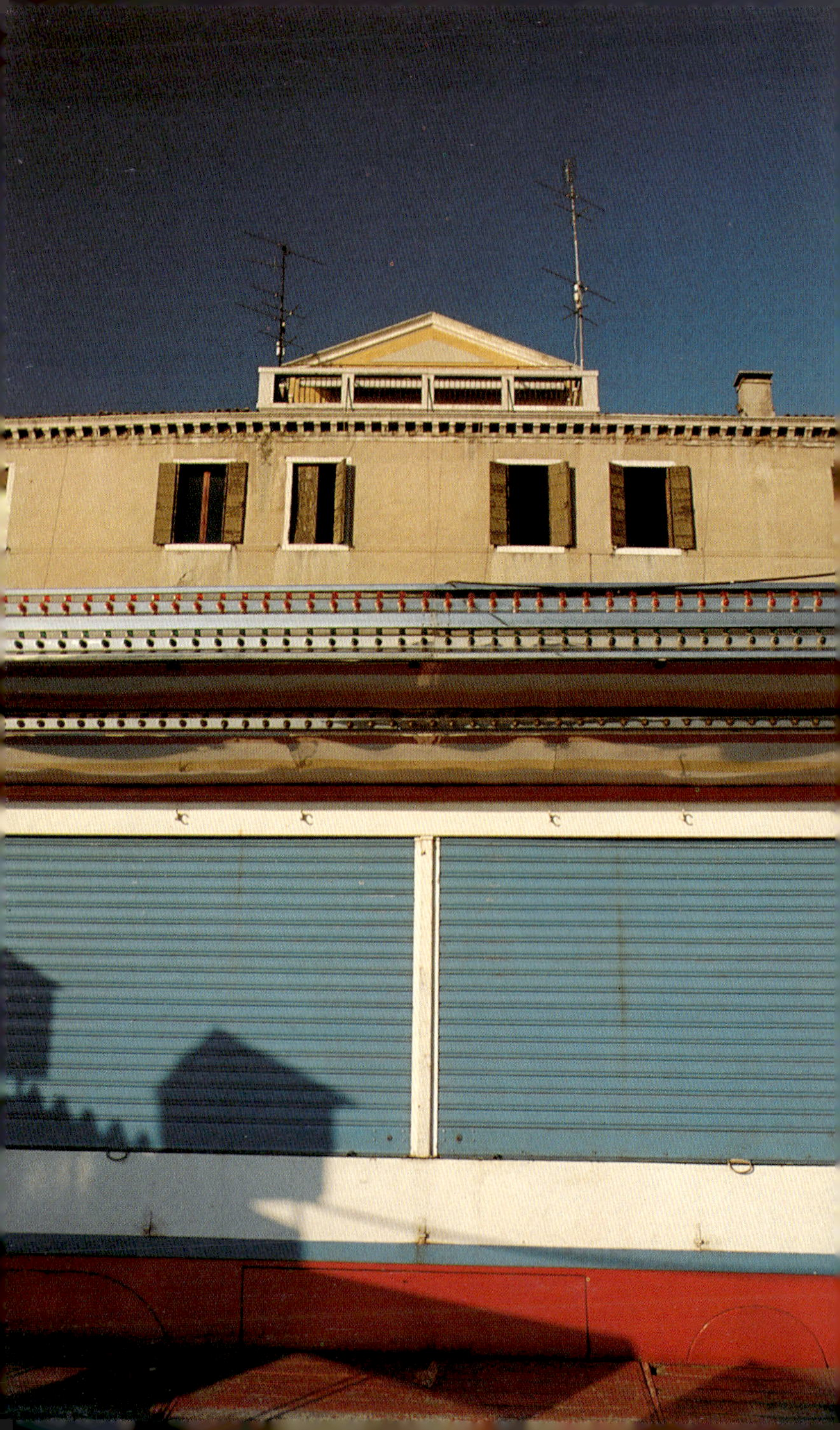

bellows available for the Minolta 9000!) or for users of the stop-down button (see "Depth of Field Control"), which is only used to assess depth of field. This is due to optical geometry and not to image brightness.

The so-called "Acute Matt Screen" has a similar effect to that of the microprism ring with a clearly defined transition from unsharp to sharp. This screen surface contains also a great number of these tiny flat microprisms (over 32000 per screen). However, the grain structure is no longer apparent, only the sharpness transition, and for this reason its suitability does not depend on the lens aperture.

Sharpness in Practical Application

Focusing, either by autofocus or manually, has one purpose – to adjust the lens so that the image of the targeted object projected on the film is as sharp as possible. If the lens is set to depict an object in sharp focus at 5m distance from the camera, then this does not imply that an object at 4.9m would suddenly be unsharp. The sharpness decreases gradually in front of and behind the focused plane. The unsharpness is noticed only from a certain distance range – the so-called depth of field. This spatial depth also bridges any inaccuracies in AF-focusing. The extent of the depth of field depends on the working aperture, the distance of the object and the lens focal length. This means we have several tools at our disposal for controlling the depth of field.

What should be sharp and what should not be sharp? Our

Because of the angle of view of the telephoto lens, spatially distant objects (from each other and the camera) may be brought closer to the viewer and each other. The impression of depth is suppressed as the objects are "bunched" closer together because of the smaller difference in scale of far off objects. The telephoto perspective produces a flatter, two-dimensional effect.　　　　　*Photo: Jürgen Lehr*

eyes continuously scan all details around us and we gain the impression that all our surroundings are at all times in sharp focus. But the human eye has not only optical but also psychological limitations that restrict depth of field. We see only what we concentrate on, all other details being suppressed by actual unsharpness and by subjective non-attention.

This concentration on only subjectively important details is also an important tool in pictorial photography. We are able to convey the same impression by limiting the depth of field. This means moving as close as possible to the subject and selecting an aperture/shutter speed combination, manually if necessary if the AF mechanism does not produce the right results, so that the main subject is shown

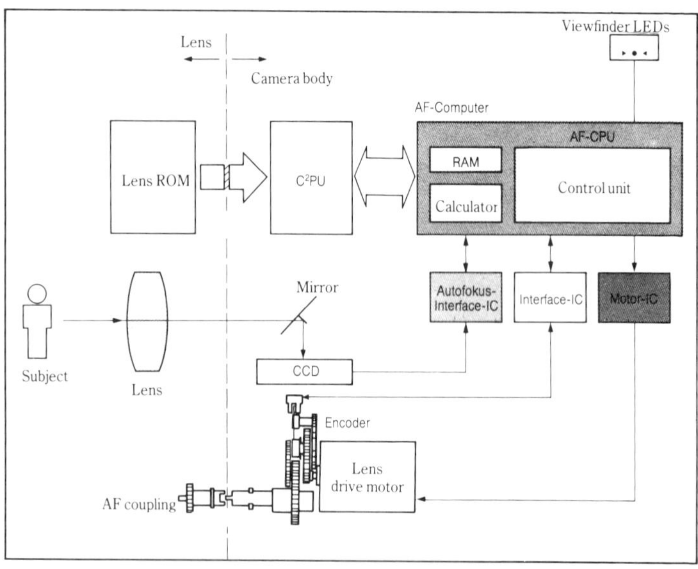

This diagramatic representation of the AF system shows which modular parts correspond in order that the Minolta 9000 can quickly and safely set the focus. A special flashgun may be connected to the control circuit to allow automatic focusing even in the dark.

against a blurred background. This may easily be assessed in the viewfinder: the aperture is completely open during focusing and the depth of field is therefore the smallest for the attached lens. It is possible to emphasise this effect by changing to a longer focal length lens. What is important, though, is to expose at a large aperture. Generally this should present no problem, except with very fast films in bright daylight. Using an average speed film in average outdoor lighting conditions the fastest shutter speed of $1/4000$ second should easily allow an aperture of f/2.8. If the lens has a larger aperture, then use it if possible.

In many situations the opposite is desirable. The depth of field is needed to be as large as possible to accommodate, for example, a group of people in the foreground, against the backdrop of a lovely landscape. The solution is again dependent on several factors:

○ If the people or the foreground details convey the important message, then it will be necessary to reproduce the background with a certain degree of unsharpness. Therefore you focus on the foreground, either by AF or manually, store this setting by the focusing lock if the foreground is to be presented off-centre; then you select a large or average aperture to take the shot.

○ The foreground and figures are only incidental detail but both the foreground and the background are to be shown in sharp focus. In this typical landscape with figures shot you use a wide-angle lens (e.g. 24mm or 28mm) and move a sufficient distance from the subject. This should produce a sufficiently large depth of field even with average aperture values.

○ Finally you are faced with the problem of having to show everything in sharp focus from a relatively close range (say 1m) to the middle distance (say 10m). As an example take an interior shot in a room. In this case the depth of field at close range may be ensured by the selection of a small aperture and a correspondingly slow shutter speed, possibly also a wide-angle lens, which may be necessary anyway because of restricted space. The camera will have to be supported on a tripod or at least a table-top tripod.

In order to control the depth of field the aperture has to be controlled. This means either in aperture priority mode or perhaps in MANUAL. In the first case the aperture is set by operating either the shutter speed switch or the aperture switch, in the second case only by the aperture switch. (See chapter "Principles of Exposure") It is also possible to control the aperture (via program shift) in shooting mode PROGRAM, but this is cumbersome. The best way is to use A-mode which is designed for aperture preselection.

Depth of Field Control

The range and extent of the depth of field may be ascertained either visually or by consulting a scale on the lens. The aperture stop-down lever on the inner side of the grip, to the right of the Minolta 9000, serves for visual assessment of depth of field. To use this facility switch the camera on and swing the lever from its resting position out towards the grip and push about half a centimetre down. Now the aperture will stop down to the manually or automatically selected aperture, regardless in what shooting mode the camera is at the moment. The image in the viewfinder will darken at the same time, by how much depends on the size of the aperture. The depth of field seen in the viewfinder now corresponds to that of the final photograph. For small working apertures the image in the viewfinder will be rather dark and the assessment of the depth of field will be difficult as a consequence.

Depressing the lever fully downwards will return the aperture to its largest opening. Exposure metering and control is inactivated in this state; in the LCD field the "F" of the aperture display will blink. If you wish to compare the effect for several different aperture settings you will have to open the aperture, select a new setting, and then stop down again to check the effect.

The second and much quicker way of assessing the depth of field is to check the depth of field indicator on the lens. This is the scale on top of the·lens, immediately beneath the distance scale window, consisting of thin lines arranged on both sides of the bold distance setting index. One pair of thin lines are associated with certain aperture values, i.e. (for lens f/1.4/50) the two innermost line markers for f/4, and then f/8, f/16 and f/22. For a certain aperture and distance setting the zone of sharpness extends from the distance read off above the left line marker of the selected aperture value up to the corresponding distance above the right line marker. If, for example, the standard 50mm lens is set at 2m (white distance scale) and you wish to know the depth of field at this distance with f/8 as the aperture setting, then you read the line marker above the aperture value "8" on the left, which should be at about 1.7m, and then the line marker above the aperture value "8" on the right, which reads 2.5m. The depth of field in this case will therefore extend from 1.7 to 2.5m.

Conversely it is possible to read the distance and aperture ranges for a required depth of field range. If you need to show an object in sharp focus between 2m and 5m, then you turn the setting ring on the lens after switching from AF to M on the camera, until the distance markers 2 and 5 align with the pair of depth of field markers. In this example the distance values will indicate an aperture value between f/8 and f/16, i.e. aperture f/11. You have to remember the values of the intermediate stops, the scale is not physically large enough to show all the values. This corresponds to a distance value of 2.75m (this has also to be assessed) above the bold setting index as the correct distance setting.

Two further points should be noted on the subject of the depth of field indicator. Firstly, only lenses with fixed focal length have such an indicator: zoom lenses do not. This is due to the fact that the depth of field depends on the focal length of the lens and as this is variable with a zoom lens, the scales required to represent the change across varying focal lengths would be much too complicated and impossible to accomodate considering the structural arrangement of the Minolta Zoom lenses.

Secondly, the range indications should not be taken as precise indications. Even the distance markers are only approximations. The scale is not linear, therefore the intermediate values are difficult to assess. These markings are given to indicate whether you would note any unsharpness when looking at the picture. And this is purely a subjective assessment whose precision can hardly be said to be greater than that of the indicator.

Finally, we seldom spend much time in considering the depth of field whilst the autofocus motor whirrs away, following the subject. Personally I find that, despite its somewhat cumbersome procedure, it is still best to use the stop-down lever to check the depth of field, should this be necessary from time to time.

Sharpness and Movement

Sharpness is not only dependent on exact focusing, it also depends on the shutter speed. One possible source of unsharpness could be camera shake at the time of shutter release, another is movement of the subject itself. If the subject being photographed moves, then it is obvious that the image projected on the film will also move. Now we are left with the question of how to reduce this effect by increasing the shutter speed far enough to keep the resulting unsharpness within acceptable tolerances so that it is not noticeable as blur.

Whatever the criterion, the object moving in front of the lens should produce as little movement on the film as possible. Any movements or blur should not be recognizable in the print, nor even in enlargements. The movement in the picture depends on the one hand on the reproduction ratio (focal length of the lens and distance to the subject), and on the other on the speed of subject and shutter speed. The variable that we need to control is the shutter speed, and this may be calculated according to equations or read off from tables. It is rarely the case that you have time during shooting to consult tables or take out your calculator to work out formulae. I shall provide some quick guidelines: using a focal length of 50mm and taking a subject at 50m distance moving at 50km/h, you should take the shot at $^1/_{250}$ second to obtain satisfactory sharpness. This applies to a movement at right angles to the lens axis.

Taking this basic value, you can vary it according to different circumstances. Longer focal lengths require a shorter exposure time: therefore $^1/_{500}$ second for a 105mm

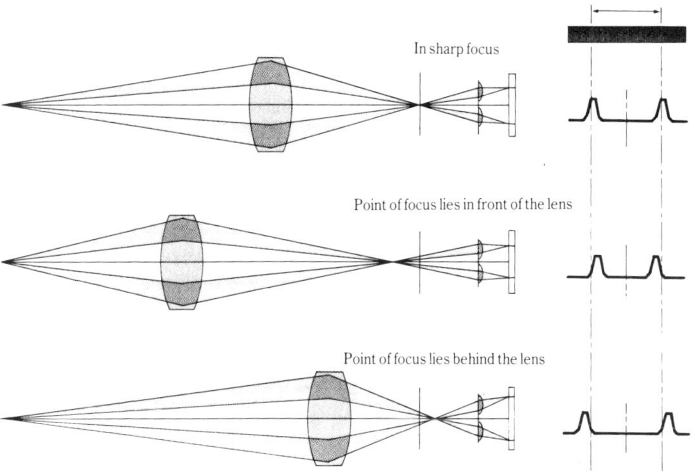

The camera compares the metered data with reference values and is thus able to assess whether the lens setting is too far or too close.

focal length, $^1/_{750}$ second at 135mm (intermediate shutter speed values are sometimes possible in A-mode) and $^1/_{1000}$ second at 200mm or 210mm (zoom lenses), etc. Slower subject movements allow longer exposure times e.g. $^1/_{125}$ second at 25 km/h. The subject distance on the other hand has the opposite effect: moving closer, to 25m for example, will necessitate doubling the shutter speed as well, i.e. again $^1/_{500}$ second. If the object moves diagonally to the lens axis, then the shutter speed may be halved ($^1/_{125}$ second instead of $^1/_{250}$ second). If the object moves directly towards or away from the camera then the exposure time may even be quadrupled ($^1/_{60}$ second). You may work out similar rules for other movements, based on these guidelines.

Unless you opt for intentional movement blur (see next chapter) you should always choose the fastest possible shutter speed under the prevailing lighting conditions when shooting moving objects. In good light and using a relatively fast film you are often in a position to attain even the fastest shutter speed of $^1/_{4000}$ second that the Minolta 9000 shutter can offer. In sports photography and similar situations many professional photographers choose a fast shutter speed (i.e. $^1/_{1000}$ second) and rely then on the shutter speed priority for correct exposure.

If the circumstances do not allow such fast shutter speeds then there are still a few tricks to catch moving objects with longer times. Moving the camera in time with an object that is in itself unchanged by its own movement, e.g. a racing car, would show the racing car in sharp focus, while the background would be even more blurred. This method, called "panning", emphasises the dramatic effect of the fast movement by the blurred unsharpness of the background. Taking subjects with uneven movements (sprinters, racing horses) then you have to accept the movement blur of the arms and legs for example as an expression of the speed. Certain types of movement may be caught at the so-called "dead point" – i.e. an athlete in high jump at the highest point of the jump is momentarily still and it is possible to catch this particular moment even with a relatively slow shutter speed.

Controlled Unsharpness

Similar to selective and intentional restriction of depth of field it is possible to improve the impact of a picture by intentional movement blur. This is the case in the previous example of panning the racing car against the exaggeratedly blurred background. Another situation may be a child waiting on the curb against the traffic's movement (taken at, say, $^1/_{30}$ second) conveying the impression of the little isolated creature trapped within the anonymous furious speed of everyday life.

Unsharpness is also relative from a different point of view. The subjectively admissible loss in detail depends, amongst other factors, on how much detail the subject has to offer. A large object, perhaps a plane taking off, requires a relatively large degree of unsharpness to convey its speed. One could also say that a slight degree of unsharpness is hardly discernible in the case of the enormous bulk of the aircraft. Compared with this the unsharpness of fine, well lit structures, e.g. a delivery van with delicate writing on its side, would be noticed a lot more.

A similar situation is the out-of-focus fine structure of a sunlit facade of a building, which would be considered unacceptable. However, if the same facade were taken as a shapeless outline in hazy fog it could be shown at an even greater degree of unsharpness and still be acceptable. The only important criterion in all these cases is that the intentional unsharpness enhances the pictorial impact.

All About Lenses

Any self-respecting SLR camera outfit has to incorporate a reasonable range of lenses. The lenses are part of the system. They offer the possibility of controlling the angle of view and scale of reproduction of a subject, as well as the perspective, by the alternative effects of focal length or distance. These controlling factors can be assessed very effectively by means of the SLR focusing screen.

The two key terms here are the focal length and the shooting distance. Using a 50mm lens the head of a person 2m distant from the lens is represented as about 5mm high on the film. The same head taken from .the same distance, but with a 135mm lens, would bring the head to 13.5mm high on the negative. Using a 24mm lens the head would be only 2.5mm. If you wanted to represent the head at a height of 5mm, still using the 24mm lens, then you would have to move closer to the subject, to about 1m distance. This might not be very flattering for a portrait though. (see "Principles of Perspective").

On the other hand, if a subject is shown smaller in the negative although the shooting distance has not been increased, you will be able to accommodate more in the frame. The angle of view is larger for shorter focal lengths. However, the quality of the lens will determine the reproduction of the fine detail.

The human eye covers an angle of view of about 70°, or even 80° if we consider the total sweep of both eyes without turning the head. The 50mm lens on the other hand, which is considered the standard lens, covers only 39°. If we wish to show in a picture all that we can see by the sweep of our eyes, perhaps an expansive landscape or a skyscraper, then we shall need the wide-angle lens. Minolta offers the 28mm covering a angle of view of 65° and the 24mm with a angle of view of 73°.

The longer focal lengths offer a narrower view, like a telescope. The Minolta 135mm covers a horizontal angle of view of 15° and the 600mm as little as 3.5°. The relative reproduction scales are 2.7-times to 12-times that of the 50mm standard lens.

Zoom or Fixed Focus Lenses

Changing the lens avoids changing the shooting position. This is even more true of zoom lenses.

Variable focal length lenses have certain advantages and certain disadvantages compared with fixed focal length lenses. The great advantage lies of course in their versatility. A variable focal length range of three to four times of that of a fixed focal length, even five times if we consider the 28mm-135mm, covers a considerable range of traditional fixed focal lengths. If, for example, you invest in only two lenses, the 28-85mm and the 75-300mm zoom lenses, you will cover the entire focal length range, apart from the extreme wide-angle of 24mm and telephoto of 600mm of this Minolta system. When I take my Minolta 9000 out I usually carry these two zoom lenses and the 24mm wide-angle lens and find that I am well equipped for almost every situation.

The exact assessment of the field of view seen through the viewfinder is part of the system's flexibility; in fact the use of zoom lenses became feasible only after the introduction of SLR camera construction. Looking through the viewfinder will show you exactly how the field of view changes with changing focal length and you can choose exactly that setting which will provide the desired frame for your shot. Fixed focal length lenses cannot offer such continuous adjustment.

Zoom lenses have other facilities to offer, and seven of the fifteen lenses in this Minolta system are variable focal length lenses. If you prefer to use a lighter lens, then you may accept a smaller range (35-70mm and 100-200mm) for the weight advantage. Or if you never use a lens longer than 135mm, then you can cover the entire range that is useful to you by the 28-135mm zoom lens. I shall discuss the various alternatives in zoom lenses later under "Zoom Lenses".

Fixed focal length lenses are generally better in their optical performance, but the difference is hardly noticeable with many modern lenses and assumes importance only in very large-scale enlargements. The only real disadvantage of zoom lenses is their slower speed, the largest aperture usually lies at about f/3.5 or f/4.5. The largest aperture value often varies with changing focal length and is even smaller for longer focal lengths but the exposure metering and control takes care of this automatically. When shooting outside in good lighting conditions or when using a fast film, this usually presents no real problem. The professional photographer tends to reach for the fixed focal length lens only if the lighting conditions are unfavourable. It is possible to find fast zoom lenses, but these tend to be prohibitively expensive, and very heavy.

However, generally speaking it is more practical to photograph with zoom lenses, especially in the middle range of the focal lengths. Apart from the standard and macro 50mm lenses, there are no other fixed focal length lenses between 28mm and 135mm that are offered at present for the Minolta 9000.

Practical Perspective

The scale of reproduction in the photograph, i.e. the size at which an object is projected, depends on the distance of the subject and the focal length of the lens. One might assume therefore that the result would be the same for a subject taken close up and the same subject taken from a greater distance but with a longer focal length lens. In both cases the subject would appear the same size on the film. Indeed this will be the case for two-dimensional subjects, but as soon as the subject has spatial depth, i.e. various points in it are at varying distances from the lens, then the result will be different. This is due to various effects: different combinations of distance and focal length are represented in different ways. It is these differences that determine the perspective of the photograph.

If, for example, we take a 6m high tree with a 50mm lens from 10m distance, then the tree will be 30mm high in the negative. A second tree 20m from the lens, will be only 15mm high, i.e. only half the height of the other. Using a 24mm lens the two trees will be 14mm and 7mm high. Moving closer to the trees with the 24mm lens, the first tree will be 30mm high at a distance of 4.8m. But the second tree, now nearly 15m away, will be only 10mm high, only a third of the size of the first.

If we now change to a 200mm telephoto, or perhaps the 100-200mm zoom lens, we can represent the first tree 30mm high on the negative by moving 40m away. The farther tree, still 10m behind the first, is now 50m distant from the lens, but its projection in the negative is 24mm. Using a telephoto lens will show distant objects at an apparently shorter distance from each other than taking the same objects from a shorter distance with a wide-angle lens.

The greater the relative difference in size of far away objects in the picture, the more will the perspective be emphasised and the greater the impression of depth. The closer one reaches for a far-away subject with a longer focus lens, the greater the "bunching" effect. This applies equally to trees, such as in a tree-lined avenue, and to portraits. At very short distances, usually possible only with a wide-angle lens, the parts of the face closer to the camera, such as the nose and chin, appear exceptionally large compared with the neck and ears. This exaggeration can by no means be considered beautiful, but it is correct according to the laws of optics. If the proportions of the face are to be natural, then you have to move away from your subject (2-3m or 6-9ft) and represent the face at a larger scale by using a longer lens.

The perspective depends only on the distance to the subject, the scale of reproduction on the other hand depends as well on the focal length of the lens. Therefore if we move closer to the subject and reduce the reproduction scale by using a wide-angle lens, then the impression of depth will be increased by emphasising the foreground compared with the middle distance and background. This applies to any subject. For example, a car taken close-up with exaggerated bonnet may look like a formula 1 sports car, the same model taken from a greater distance will revert to the appearance of an ordinary family saloon. The camera does not lie, but it does a good job of deceiving you!

The longer lenses would not be required for reasons of perspective alone. Enlarging the appropriate section from a picture taken by a short focus lens from the same camera position would show the same perspective. But the enlarged section will lose in quality through larger grain and lower resolution and sharpness. Thus the effects of the various focal length lenses on the chosen section of the view can be used in every case to ensure the best possible utilization of the available negative area.

Because wide-angle pictures capture a wider field with their shorter focal lengths, which would otherwise only be possible by building up a panoramic view by combining several shots, one should view the resulting picture in similar fashion, i.e. wide-angle projection of slides seen from close-up. Otherwise the subject will seem smaller than in reality and will also appear to be distorted because of the incorrect viewing distance. This is the reason why wide-angle shots are considered to produce exaggeration of the perspective. The large viewing angle covers a great extent of the depth, from very close up to far away, and objects at different distances from the camera are represented at markedly different representation scales. Viewing a wide-angle shot from a close enough distance will diminish the impression of perspective distortion. In fact a simple rule to remember is that the correct viewing distance for natural looking perspective is equal to $f \times M$ where f is the focal length of the camera lens and M the linear magnification of the final image.

Telephoto perspective is the exact opposite of wide-angle perspective. Because of the smaller differences in scale the impression of depth between closer and farther objects is suppressed. Near and far objects will appear close together. This is the well-known "bunching" effect, which may be used to good effect in picture creation. This effect cannot be counteracted by the choice of a suitable viewing distance because you would have to move so far away that you would hardly be able to see the view at all. That is hardly the point of the exercise, after all the reason why we use long focus lenses is to bring objects from a distance, such as animals, sports scenes, etc., close to the viewer.

The Minolta AF-Lens System

The lens system for the Minolta 9000 is unique in one respect. On the one hand all lenses are equipped with a mechanical coupling that connects the lens to the camera's integrated focusing motor, and on the other hand each lens has a ROM (Read-Only-Memory) chip that feeds the camera's electronic exposure program with information on focal length, aperture value limits and other information. This means that only Minolta AF-lenses can be used with this camera. Not even other Minolta lenses and, unlike other makes and models, no lenses from other manufacturers are yet suitable. Conversely, the Minolta AF-system lenses will only fit Minolta cameras with AF facility. These are at the moment the models in the 1000 series: 5000, 7000 and 9000.

The table on page 181 contains comparative values and details of Minolta AF-lenses and the subsequent section deals with practical and other characteristics of handling the camera. First a few remarks on the table.

The stated focal lengths are nominal focal lengths, the actual focal length may vary within +/- 5% of the stated value. This means that a standard 50mm lens may have an effective focal length of somewhere between 48 and 52mm. The same applies to the focal length limits of the zoom lenses.

The given lens speeds are also nominal values within acceptable tolerances. The lens speed range stated for some zoom lenses means that the speed of the lens declines with increasing focal length. This effect is automatically taken into account by the exposure program of the Minolta 9000 as also are any tolerances in the nominal speed of the lens.

The angle of view is the theoretical angle covered by the lens. This means the angle in the subject space, in front of the lens, and not in the picture space behind the lens. The literature accompanying most equipment states the viewing angle of the lens in terms of the diagonal angle of view. This makes the lens specification appear more impressive, in particular if we are talking about wide-angle lenses. However, we are interested in the

---

For this shot, autofocus was used to make sure the fountain was critically sharp with the near flowers pleasantly out of focus to emphasise the impression of depth. Spot metering on the flowers ensured a satisfactory exposure. *Photo: Joachim F. Richter*

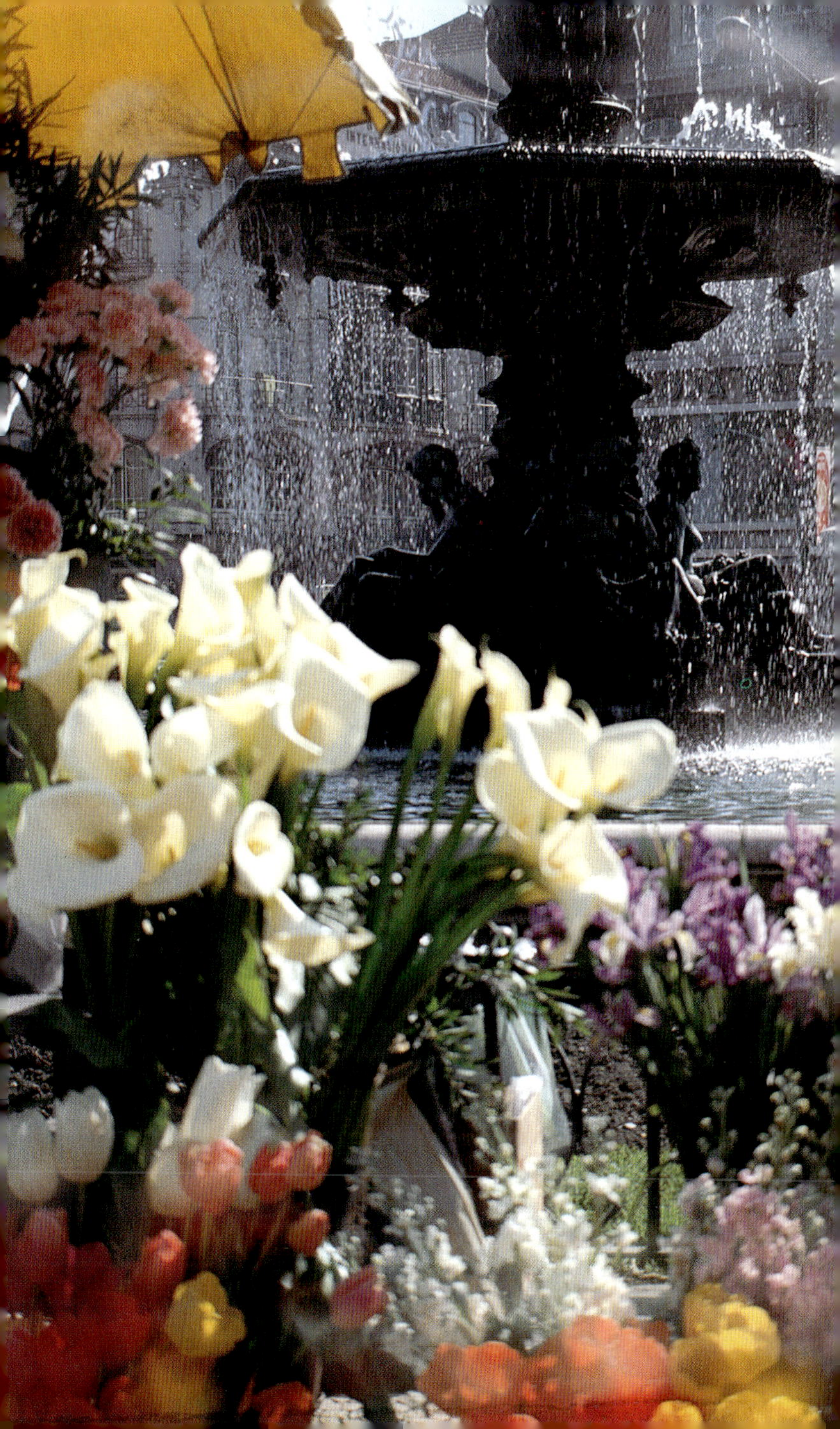

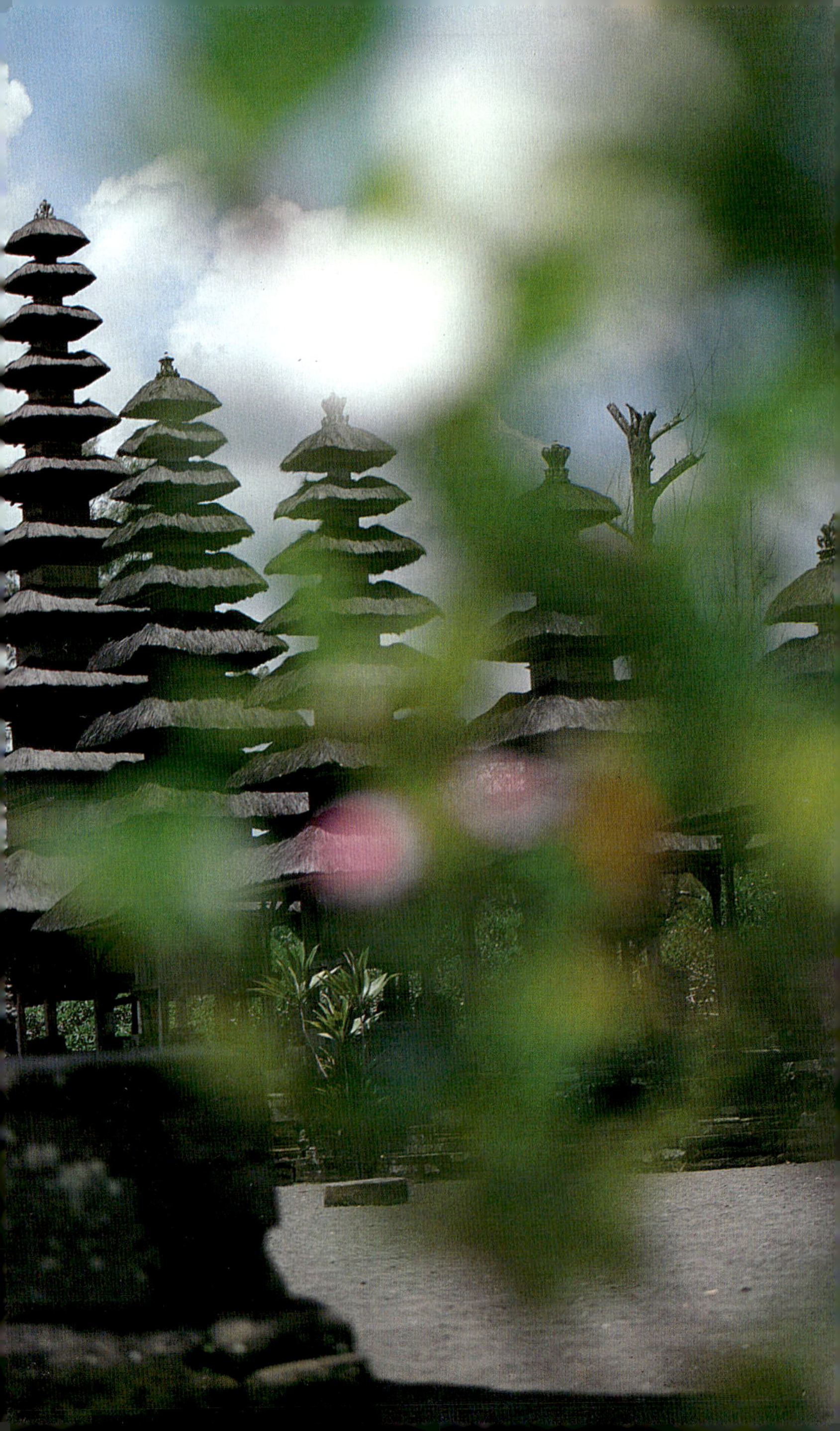

horizontal as well as in the vertical viewing angle of a lens, i.e. the space covered from side to side and from top to bottom. There are some more practical considerations. This angle is the angle at infinity setting and gets smaller for closer distances, especially in the close range up to macro range. However, this has hardly any effect in practical applications as the actual field of view may be assessed in the viewfinder. Another point is that the angle refers to the nominal focal length and the film frame format 24×36mm. What is seen through the viewfinder, as with slide frames and frame masks for enlargers, is a slightly smaller format of 23×35mm. But as such extremely precise definitions have little practical effect, we accept the somewhat generalized specification.

The smallest aperture value of the lens is usually stated in brackets after the lens speed value. This information is contained in the ROM chip and fed to the camera's electronics where it is used to determine the limiting values for aperture settings and for display in the LCD window and in the data field in the viewfinder.

The structure of the lens (number of individual elements "L" and groups "G") is not as important as an indication of quality in a modern lens as it was for previous generations when the quantity of glass expended was equivalent to the degree of optical correction. Today the quality of a lens depends a lot more on the type of glass used and the structural characteristics. Zoom lenses need more elements in their construction than fixed focal length lenses, because of the variable focal length and the consequent optical aberrations. All lenses are coated, i.e. the glass/air

---

Subjects like this should not be left to automatic focusing. The camera cannot decide which of the two main objects should be sharp. The sharp/unsharp effect in the facing picture was achieved with a telephoto lens and a large aperture coupled with manual focusing on the distant buildings. *Photo: Joachim F. Richter*

surfaces have a coating that supresses reflections, increasing the transmission of the glass and increasing colour saturation.

The close-up limit is the shortest manual distance setting on the lens, measured from the subject to the film plane (ca 6mm in front of the rear surface of the back panel of the camera, or 44.5mm behind the lens flange). For most lenses the close-up limit is also the shortest distance setting for automatic focusing. Some zoom lenses have a macro range that is only adjustable manually (see section "Macro Lenses"). The close-up range stated in the table is the macro limit.

The greatest scale is the reproduction scale for the shortest focusing distance, with macro setting, where available.

Dimensions: the physical length refers to the distance from the lens front edge without lens cap to the flange bezel, without the part that protrudes into the interior of the camera. Furthermore, it refers to the lens set at infinity and in the case of zoom lenses to the focal length with the shortest extension (this is usually not the shortest focal length). The diameter is the largest diameter, e.g. the broadest front part of the 300mm and 600mm lenses. The filter diameter refers to the diameter of the front thread; in the case of the 300mm and 600mm lenses the filters are attached by slide-in holder in the tube.

Fixed Focal Lengths

The 24mm f/2.8 has the greatest angle of view of all lenses in the Minolta AF range. It is also one of the two focal lengths not covered by any of the zoom lenses. This true wide-angle lens is supplied with a special lens hood and is particularly suitable for landscape photography, interior shots, architecture, etc. A special structural

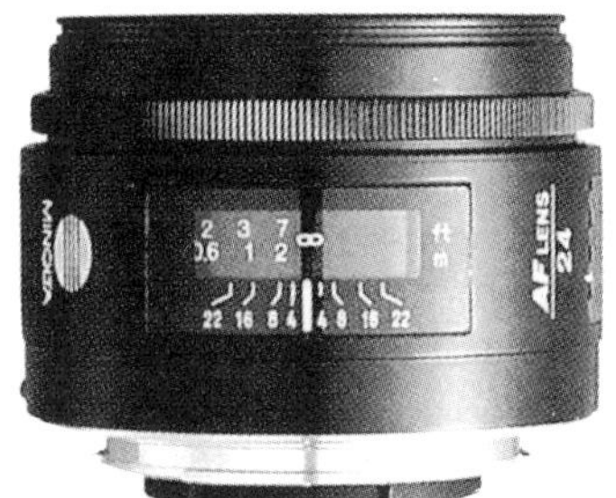

The AF f/2.8 24mm, a lens between the super wide-angle and the wide-angle range. The large viewing angle is ideal for general view shots, even if the subject details are presented on a rather small scale.

characteristic of this lens is the focusing by internal adjustment of the rear elements; the overall length of the lens extension remains constant.

The 28mm f/2.8 is a normal wide-angle lens and is useful as an additional lens in the wide-angle range for those who wish to make do with one of the lighter zoom lenses in the average focal length range (e.g. the 35-105mm). The 28-85mm and the 28-135mm cover this focal length but the 28mm fixed focus lens is lighter, convenient to carry and use and has a bigger maximum aperture.

The 50mm f/1.4 is the traditional standard lens for the modern 35mm SLR camera, and it is also the fastest lens in the Minolta AF series. Four of the zoom lenses offered by Minolta cover this focal length, so it may not be necessary to purchase this lens which is often sold together with the camera (see section "What

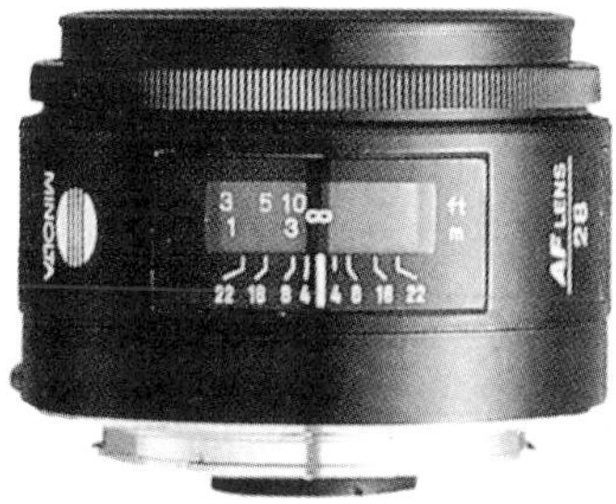

The AF f/2.8 28mm, a good all-round wide-angle lens, useful for snapshots, architecture and landscape photography.

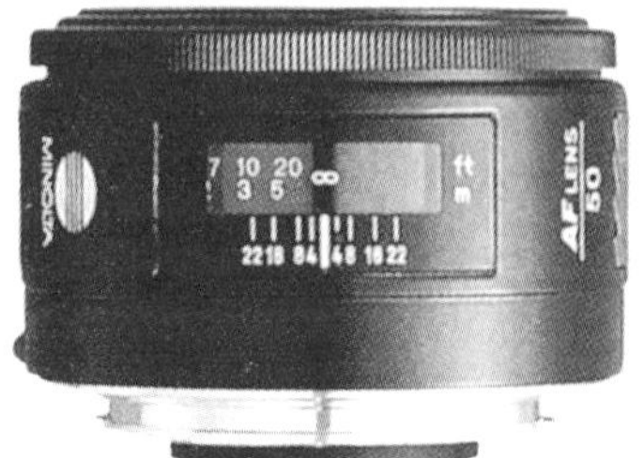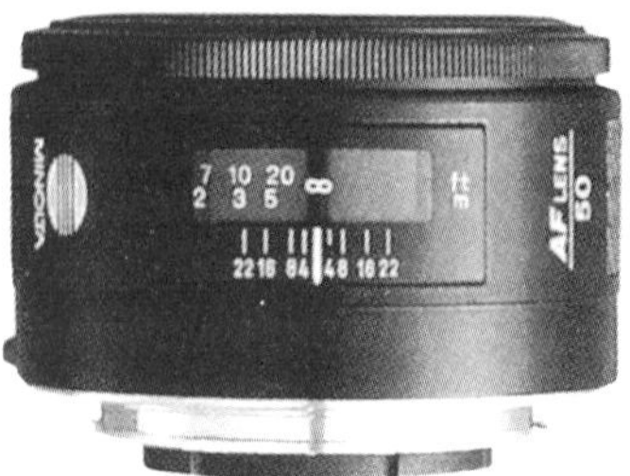

Often dismissed as boring, but universally useful: the standard 50mm lenses: AF f/1.4 50mm and AF f/1.7 50mm.

Equipment?"). However, those of you who often photograph in poor lighting conditions will be very glad of the great speed that this lens has to offer.

The 50mm f/1.7 is the cheaper alternative to the f/1.4 which costs about 50% more for the half-stop increase in lens speed. The practical advantage of the fast f/1.4 is questionable. I should say it's rather a question of prestige. That Minolta offer both these speeds for the 50mm is a matter of marketing policy. The two 50mm lenses are the cheapest in the Minolta AF series.

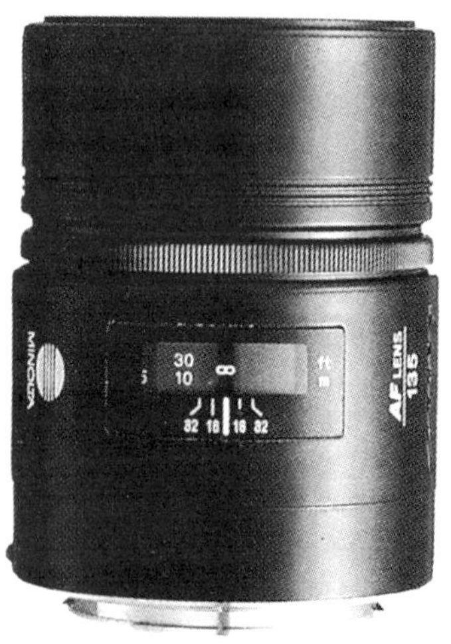

The AF f/2.8 135mm. A short telephoto which is still useful for portrait photography and to bridge distances optically. Also useful for selecting detail from a larger subject.

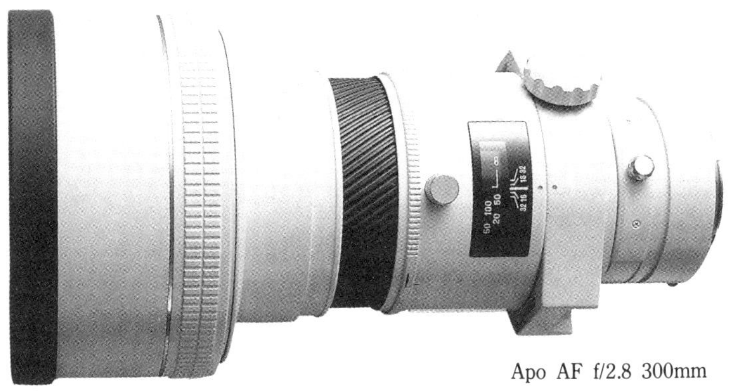

Apo AF f/2.8 300mm

The 50mm f/2.8 Macro will be described later in the section "Macro Lenses".

The 135mm f/2.8 complements one of the short zooms (e.g. the 28-85mm or the 35-105mm), but it is also very handy as special equipment for applications such as, for example, portraits. It has internal focusing, i.e. the lens elements move against each other for distance setting, and the length of the lens remains constant during focusing. Internal focusing is particularly suitable for automatic focusing because the power needed to move the internal elements is less than would be required to move the entire lens barrel.

The 300mm f/2.8 is the first of the "big guns" in the Minolta AF system. This is a very extravagant lens, mainly because of its great speed, and it is particularly suitable for professional sports and animal photography, reportage, etc. Apart from the hefty price, its weight at 2.5kg must also be described as such. The 300mm focal length can also be attained by the 75-300mm zoom lens, but at the cost of two whole aperture stops.

Similarly to the 135mm lens, the 300mm f/2.8 has internal focusing. In order to reduce the autofocusing time it is possible to limit the setting range. To do this you set the white ring immediately in front of the focusing window such that the setting screw forms a stop at the required distance setting. The automatic focusing will now move between this stop and either the close limit or infinity. But if the subject being photographed lies outside that range then the AF mechanism cannot function. Another feature of this lens is that the two front elements are made from the so-called AD-glass (anomalous dispersion), producing particularly good correction of colour aberrations.

Normally this lens would be used on a tripod. For this purpose a mounting ring with tripod thread is provided such that the camera with attached lens is supported more or less directly beneath its centre of gravity. The camera and lens may be turned and secured by a locking screw within the ring for horizontal and vertical format shots.

The 600mm f/4 doubles the telephoto range of the 300mm f/2.8 and weighs twice as much. This is the longest lens offered in the AF range and lies outside any of the focal lengths covered by any zoom lens. Its application is similar to that of the 300mm f/2.8. Also similar to the 300mm it is also constructed of special glasses, has internal focusing, a rotating tripod mount and distance stop for the automatic focusing range.

Zoom Lenses

The 28-85mm f/3.5-4.5 is the best compromise for a universal zoom covering the focal lengths from wide-angle to the shorter telephoto range without being too heavy. The obliquely grooved rubber covered setting ring serves for focal length adjustment; the scale on the ring shows the selected value. When shooting, this is usually not

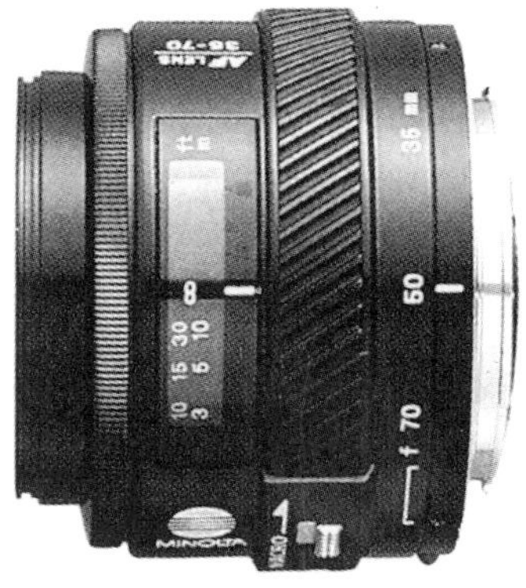

The most compact zoom lens presently available for the Minolta 9000: the 35-70mm is an extended standard lens. It has a selectable macro setting (without AF).

very important; what is important is what you can see through the viewfinder. The AF close-up range is 0.8m; on changing over to macro range the setting range goes down to 0.25m and the reproduction ratio to 1:4 (see "Macro Lenses"). In the macro range, however, focusing has to be manual.

The 28-135mm f/4-4.5 offers a wider focal length range compared to the above lens, but it weighs about 50% more and makes itself felt when dangling around one's neck. Its advantage is that it serves as a single universal zoom lens if you have no need for focal lengths 200mm and upwards. The close-up range of this lens is 1.5m and in the macro position, again at the cost of the AF setting facility, it may be manually focused down to 0.25m. This lens too has internal focusing (compare with description of 24mm lens).

The 35-70mm f/4 is the most compact of all the zoom lenses, hardly larger than the standard 50mm f/1.4. It may be considered as a standard lens with variable picture frame control. The use of aspherical elements allows good optical correction characteristics with only 6 elements, and this is the reason for its particularly light and compact construction. The lens also has a manually

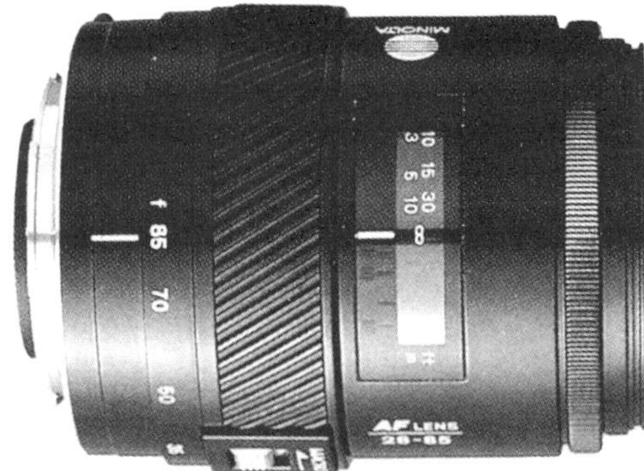

The AF f/3.5-4.5 28-85mm. A universal zoom with a leaning towards the wide-angle range; the longest focal length is ideal for portrait photography but cannot be described as a true telephoto lens.

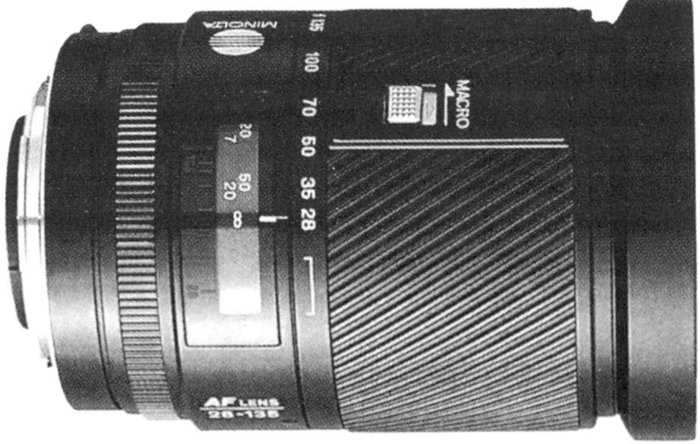

The f/4-4.5 28-135mm. A zoom lens that can replace an entire outfit, useful for a wide range of subjects.

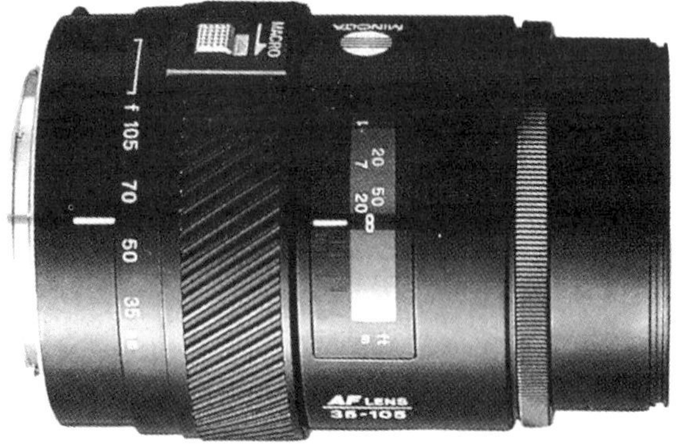

The f/3.5-4.5 35-105mm is a universal zoom just like the 28-85mm, but this time the range is shifted towards the longer focal lengths, and is therefore more restricted in the wide-angle range.

adjustable macro range down to 1m outside the AF setting range.

The 35-105mm f/3.5-4.5 corresponds in size and weight more or less to the 28-85mm lens and has similar characteristics, including the manual macro setting range. The difference is in the focal length range being shifted towards the longer telephoto range.

The 70-210mm f/4 corresponds to the most popular telephoto zoom range in SLR photography; it is also ideal in combination with either the 28-85mm or the 35-70mm. Contrary to the shorter zoom lenses, the 70-210mm has a close-up range down to the macro range (ratio 1:2.9 at a close-up limit of 1.1m at focal length 210mm) and therefore continuous AF facility.

The 75-300mm f/4.5-5.6 is only slightly larger than the above 70-210mm. Personally I find the wider focal length range very useful. Again, the macro range extends continuously in AF setting down to 1.5m (ratio 1:3.9 at 300mm). Like the 300mm and 600mm telephoto lenses, the AF setting range may be limited by a switch on the lens tube. For example, if an object is located at a

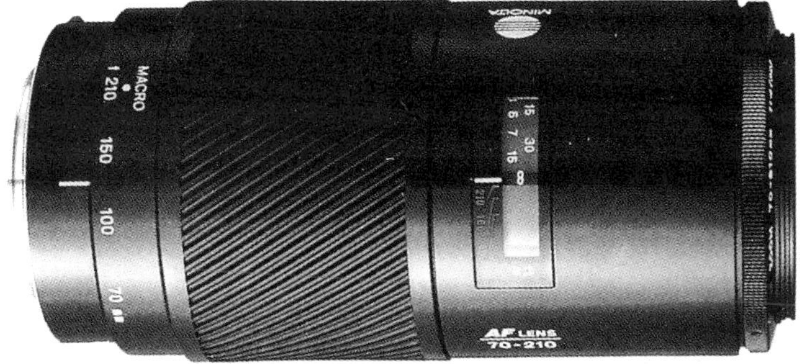

The AF f/4 70-210mm and the AF f/4 35-70mm form the ideal lens pair.

distance between 4m and infinity, then this switch is set to LIMIT which limits the focusing mechanism, AF and manual, to this range. If the switch is set to LIMIT for a closer subject, then the focusing setting will move between 1.5m and 3.3m. Switching to FULL cancels the focusing limit.

The 100-200mm f/4.5 is a very compact alternative to the 70-210mm. However you have to accept the reduced focal length range. Its advantage is that it is hardly larger or heavier than the 135mm f/2.8 telephoto lens.

What Equipment?

There are already fifteen AF lenses available and no doubt, Minolta will increase the range in the near future. You can make your choice from these lenses, as nobody needs the entire range for their personal requirements. But how do you make the choice? What are the considerations apart from the financial constraints?

Today, fixed focal length lenses may be considered special lenses for particular applications, contrary to the zoom lenses that are considered to a greater or lesser degree as universal lenses. You may consider buying a fixed focal length lens if you need the greater lens speed that these lenses invariably offer (e.g. f/1.4 of the standard 50mm lens); or if that particular focal length is not covered by one of the zoom ranges (e.g. 24mm or 600mm); or if you work regularly with a certain focal length, perhaps the 135mm for professional portrait photography; or if the particular focal length is used to complement an existing zoom range.

Most Minolta 9000 users will choose a combination of zoom lenses, perhaps complemented by some fixed focal length lenses. As mentioned previously, I find the 28-85mm and the 75-300mm are a good combination for my purposes, complemented by the 24mm f/2.8. Carrying this lot in my bag I don't get away with it particularly lightly. If you find you can do without the upper telephoto range, you could save about 500g by using the 100-200mm f/4.5 instead.

Another relatively light combination, also on the purse, is the 35-70mm and the 100-200mm. If you find the gap between 70 to 100 mm too difficult to bridge, you could choose the 35-105mm instead of the 35-70mm, but this means that you are putting a little more on the scales.

It is usual for shops to offer the camera together with one of the standard 50mm lenses. However, it is worth considering what equipment to invest in when buying the camera. The decision could easily be NOT to buy a standard 50mm lens. In Japan the 35-70mm is particularly popular as a flexible standard lens, allowing easy control of frame around the 50mm focal length. The 35-70mm is hardly any larger than the 50mm f/1.4 standard lens, weighs only 20g more, and is useful as the basis of an extended set of zoom equipment (e.g. together with the 100-200mm or the 70-210mm, as mentioned above). It is more limited than the 28-85mm and even more so than the 28-135mm, but on the other hand it is handier as a permanent fixture on the camera than one of the other heavy lumps.

Macro Lenses

The method of focusing by using a focusing screen as employed in SLR cameras is particularly advantageous for close-up shots down to the macro range. Most manufacturers of SLR cameras offer special accessories, such as extension rings, bellows and lenses corrected for the extreme close range. So far only one macro lens is available for the Minolta 9000.

This is the 50mm f/2.8 AF Macro lens and is a

standard focal length with extended focusing range, allowing a reproduction ratio of 1:1 (i.e. actual size). The unique feature is that this lens may be continuously focused by the AF facility down to its close-up limit. It possesses the usual distance scale but this should be considered as only approximate in the macro range as the AF system does not measure distance but sharpness. It also has a ratio scale. The reproduction ratios are shown on the setting ring in blue numbers from 9 to 1, i.e. 1:9, down to 1:1.

The AF facility is particularly useful and fast acting in the macro range. Correct focusing in the close-up range is well known to be rather difficult and one tends to turn the focusing ring to and fro until the object is finally in sharp focus. The AF system will do this for you much more quickly and reliably.

The ratio scale is not very exact. If the exact reproduction ratio is important, then you should use focusing screen type S. As soon as the camera and lens is set up for the shot, you place a small millimetre scale into the field of view. You can then check in the viewfinder how many millimetre intervals on the scale correspond to the millimeter divisions on the focusing screen. The result will be the reproduction ratio on the negative, the reciprocal value the magnification. If, for example, 3mm of the millimeter scale in the image field corresponds to one millimeter on the focusing screen, then the reproduction ratio is 1:3 or 0.33x.

Several of the zoom lenses can also be used in the macro range. The zoom ring has a slide switch marked "Macro" which is pushed forward whilst the zoom ring on the lens is simultaneously turned in the direction of the blue arrow, this will take you to the macro range of that lens. For the 28-85mm the macro range is to the right of the setting for 28mm.

In this distance range the focusing motor is inoperative and the adjustment has to be done manually, although

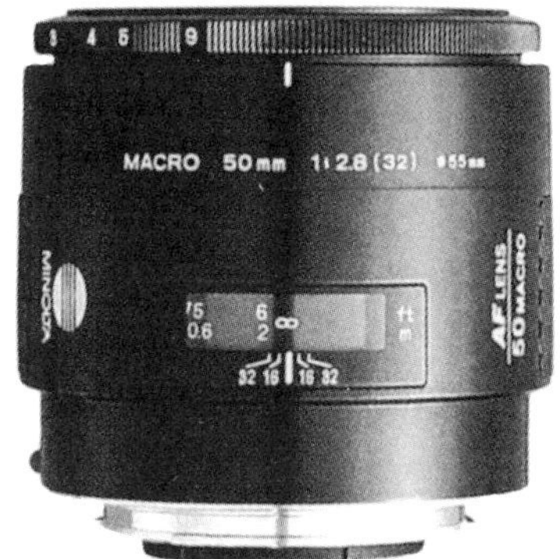

The blue numbers on the front ring of the 50mm macro lens show the reproduction scales. The fully motorized AF facility also functions in the macro range.

still assisted by the sharpness metering:

○ **Either** depress the release lightly as for focusing lock and move towards or away from the subject until the focusing check (green LED and bleep tone) indicates optimum sharpness, then release immediately. The focus setting is not stored in this mode, the display changes continuously with the focusing setting between unsharp (red arrow) and sharp (green arrow).

○ **Or** hold the camera still whilst keeping the release slightly depressed, turn the zoom ring (not the focusing ring) until the focusing check indicates correct setting.

The actual macro range depends on the type of lens attached. The macro range is set at 28mm in the case of the 28-85mm zoom lens, this means a very short subject distance. The same also applies to the 28-135mm. In the case of the 35-70mm and 35-105mm the macro range lies at the longer focal length limit, beyond 70mm and 135mm respectively, and this is often a lot more convenient for close-ups.

Finally the long zoom lenses (70-210mm and

75-300mm) have continuous setting ranges and the AF facility can therefore be used even in the macro range. The largest reproduction scale lies again at the longer limit of the focal length. These lenses are particularly handy for shooting small animals, insects, butterflies, etc., which would otherwise be scared away.

The performance in the macro range of one of these zoom lenses cannot be compared with that of a dedicated macro lens, such as the 50mm f/2.8. But this facility should be considered a bonus and it is quite adequate for many situations.

Infra-red Setting

Amateurs seldom use infra-red film. Moreover, most lenses are colour-corrected only for the visible spectrum. The Minolta AF lenses do have a correction setting for infra-red photography. In the case of fixed focal length lenses this is the red dot next to the thick white line of the distance index.

The correction setting is a little cumbersome, but IR shots are rarely hurried snapshots and this should therefore present no problem. First bring the subject into focus by either manual or AF setting, then switch to manual focusing. Note the value on the distance scale (the value or intermediate value opposite the white line on the distance scale), then turn the distance ring slightly to the right, viewed from the top, so that the noted distance is aligned with the red IR index point. Now attach the IR filter and take the shot.

For short focal length lenses the correction is only a minor one. In the case of the 50mm lens the red dot almost coincides with the line marker for the depth of field indicator of aperture f/4. Consequently you can neglect the IR correction for shots with smaller apertures than f/4 as these would lie within the depth of field.

The procedure gets a little more complicated with zoom lenses as the correction will vary with changing focal lengths. Zoom lenses therefore have several focal length related IR index markers; you have to adjust for the appropriate value. Using the 28-135mm, for example, you note the point opposite the fat red, not the white, index and adjust it to the corresponding red index marker for the selected focal length. Only the values 135 and 28mm bear legends; the intermediate values 100, 70, 50, and 35mm are indicated by line markers.

Filters

Filters are used to modify colour effects in the final photograph. These are used in particular for colour slide photography in situations when the light is too blue, such as sky light without direct sunlight on the subject, or too red (late afternoon or tungsten light), producing unwanted colour casts in the slide. For colour print film, filters are less important as any slight colour cast may be corrected during printing. Even so, initial correction when taking the photograph will ensure better quality of the mass-produced print.

The filters in this group comprise blue filters ranging from very pale to a noticeable blue, e.g. for use with daylight film in tungsten light, and the amber filters. The latter range from the almost colourless UV filters for preventing the blue casts produced by UV radiation, for example in the high Alps, via the slightly pink skylight filter for a warmer colour rendition in open shade, down to the orange conversion filters for tungsten film in daylight.

Colour filters for black-and-white film modify the reproduction of coloured objects in monochrome and convert colour contrasts, which lose their differentiation on monochrome film, into tone contrasts. A yellow filter, for example, will make the blue sky in landscape shots appear darker and show the clouds to better effect. Orange and red filters have even more dramatic effects.

Polarizing filters these suppress polarized light and reflections from non-metal reflecting surfaces in the picture, provided the filter is correctly aligned. The effect of the filter attached to the lens may be observed through the viewfinder while the filter itself is rotated. Only circularly polarizing filters may be used for the Minolta 9000 and these are always identified as such. For reasons of optical construction, linear polarizing filters are unsuitable as they lead to incorrect results both for exposure metering and AF sharpness metering.

Portrait filters: this specialized filter series by Minolta, the so-called "phase" filters, selectively modify the colour effects in portrait photography and in particular the complexion is rendered cleanly. Portraits are also softened by reducing the sometimes unwanted pin-sharp detail.

Filters for special effects: some manufacturers offer partial filters, such as graduated filters, special effect filters for highlights, sparkles and partial colour effects, to mention just a few.

Filters are screwed into the thread at the front of the lens. The Minolta AF-lenses, with three exceptions, use either 49mm or 55mm diameter filters. The exceptions are the 28-135mm zoom lens (72mm screw-in filter) and

---

The Minolta flashguns and the Macro f/2.8 50mm provide an excellent technical solution for still life photography. For difficult subjects as these antique watches the flash was rendered sufficiently diffuse by the use of a light tent.   *Photo: Joachim F. Richter*

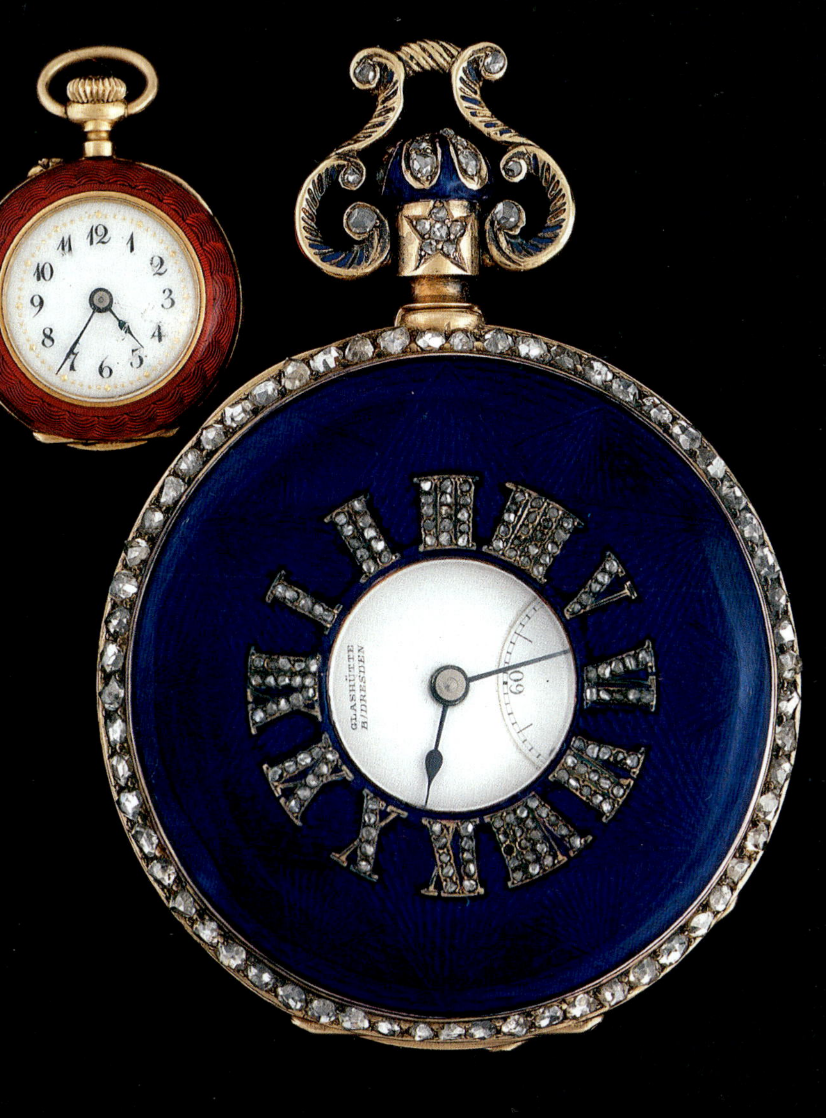
GLASHÜTTE
B/DRESDEN

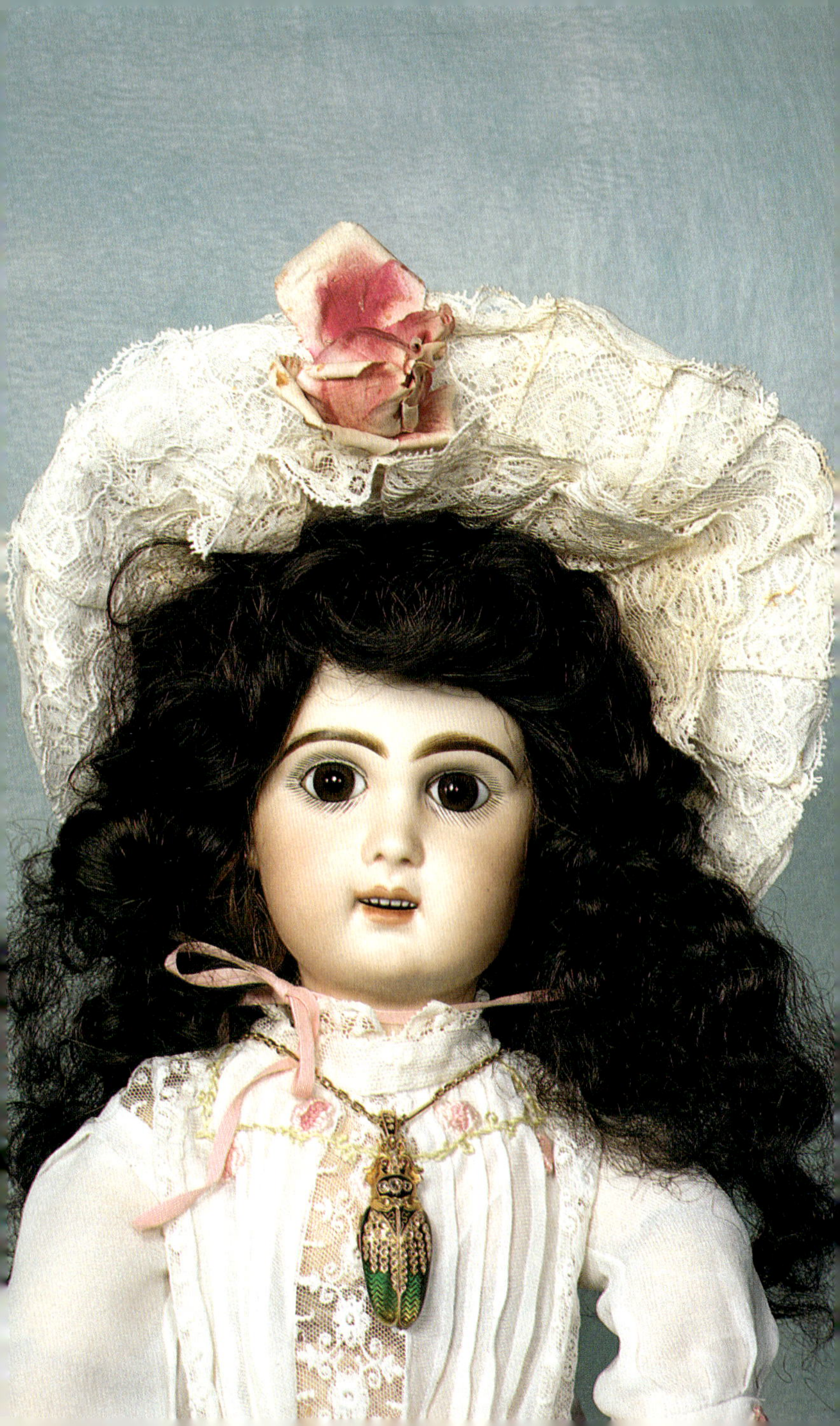

the 300mm and the 600mm Apo-lenses. The latter use 42mm filters which are inserted in a slider at the rear of the barrel. The filter would have to be enormous to fit at the front of the lens.

Filters absorb light and that means the exposure has to be increased. This is of little consequence, though, as the TTL metering will account for this automatically. It could happen that the use of filters may adversely influence the sharpness metering and may lead to incorrect results. Minolta specify that the AF facility will function perfectly with their Minolta filters L-37 (UV), 1A and 1B (skylight filters for warmer colour rendition on slide film), portrait (for portraits - see above), circular polarizing filters and colour filters for black-and-white film Y-52 (yellow), G-0 (green), O-56 (orange) and R-60 (red). If other filters are used, in particular other makes, then Minolta recommend that the filter is attached after the AF metering has been completed (switch AF off) or to focus manually in the first place.

One thing should be considered. Lenses are generally designed for a particular optical performance with reference to the glass surfaces in the system. Any additional glass elements not originally allowed for, and that also means filters, will influence the picture quality somewhat. Therefore filters of the highest quality only should be used.

Lens Hoods

A portion of the light falling on the lens is reflected by the various air/glass surfaces and finally arrives on the film as contrast-reducing stray light or flare. This effect is particularly marked when there are strong light

---

Several flashguns, connected by a CD cable and three-way adapter allow even illumination of objects in the small studio.

Photo: Joachim F. Richter

sources within or outside the image field, such as bright sun in backlit shots. These unwanted effects are partially reduced by the lens coatings but may be further reduced by protecting the lens from unwanted light entering it. For this purpose lens hoods are used. Sometimes these are built into the lens, otherwise they may be purchased separately. The shape of a lens hood is calculated for the particular focal length in order to afford sufficient protection without vignetting the image corners.

The fixed focal length lenses are equipped with built-in lens hoods, apart from the 24mm. They are pulled forward by their outer ring but for the shorter focal lengths it may be necessary to set the lens to a short distance to render the ring accessible. The 24mm wide-angle lens has a separate lens hood with bayonet fitting. This is attached to the outer ring by aligning the red marker with the red dot, and is then secured by an eighth of a turn in a clockwise direction. The wider sides (with legend) have to be at the top and bottom. The countersunk lens bezel of the 50mm Macro lens serves as a lens hood for that lens.

Separate detachable lens hoods are available for the zoom lenses, except the 28-135mm. To attach them, press the lateral buttons. The lens hoods are marked for the appropriate focal lengths. Despite the different inscriptions, the lens hoods for the two zoom lenses 70-210mm and 75-300mm are really identical. When not in use the lens hood may be reversed and kept on the lens. In this position the lens cover will also fit and the gadget bag will be less crowded. The lens hoods for the zoom lenses should be considered a compromise and care must be taken that the corners of the picture are not affected by vignetting in the wide-angle settings, and that in the telephoto setting the hood affords sufficient protection. This is the reason why there is no lens hood available for the 28-135mm: the large front element cannot be protected in the wide-angle setting.

Principles of Flash Photography

Electronic flash has been for a considerable time the most versatile artificial light source in photography. Most models and makes of flashgun have more or less elaborate facilities for automatic exposure. The TTL metering cell in the Minolta 9000 measures not only the continuous lighting conditions but also the amount of light reflected from the subject during the flash exposure. The system flashguns designed for this camera (Program Flash 4000 AF, 2800 AF and 1800 AF) control the flash duration and offer various program functions.

All these flashguns synchronise the flash down to a

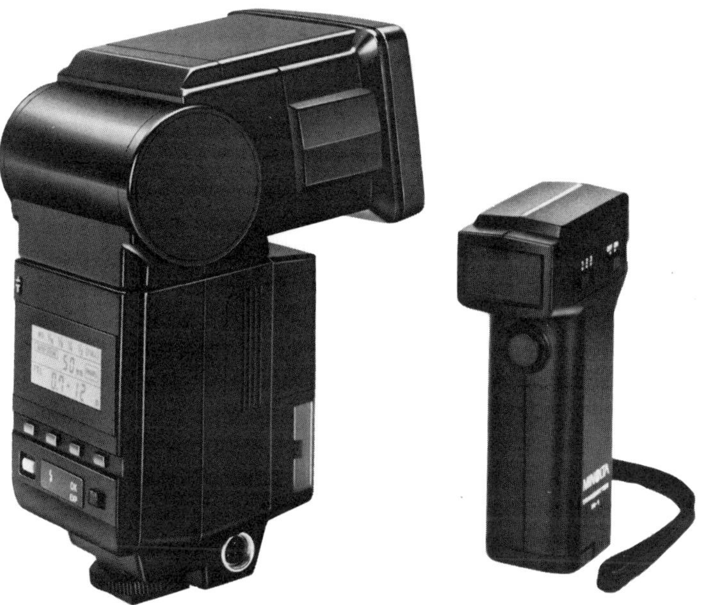

The Program Flash AF with adjustable zoom reflector. Next to it: the small handy unit of the infra-red remote release set.

fastest shutter speed of $1/250$ second. The middle contact in the accessory shoe is normally used to provide the contact for synchronization. The other contacts convey further information between camera and flashgun for various other automatic control functions.

Programmed Flash

There are various operational possibilities for Minolta system flashguns with the Minolta 9000 in all the shooting modes, usually with fully automatic exposure control.

Flash program mode (P-function) is the simplest to use. With the camera set to PROGRAM mode the aperture and shutter speed values will be set according to the program mode and the time will be somewhere between $1/60$ second and $1/250$ second. The TTL metering cell will control the flash duration. The metering will automatically account for the available light in daylight conditions and the flash will be reduced to fill-in effect.

Flash aperture priority mode (A-function), camera in shooting mode A; again, the flash duration is controlled via the TTL metering cell always according to subject luminance and preselected aperture, the synchronization time is $1/250$ second. The flash can also be used as fill-in flash.

Flash shutter speed mode (S-function), camera in shooting mode S: This is the most versatile flash mode because it is possible to control the brightness of the naturally lit background relative to that of the flash-lit subject by choice of shutter speed.

Manual flash mode (M-function), camera set to

MANUAL). This allows the choice of any available flash output and shutter speed/aperture combination.

The Program Flash 4000 AF

This instrument makes full use of the versatility that the Minolta 9000 has to offer and applies it to flash photography. Not only does it utilize this versatility, it offers a few extra refinements such as zoom reflector positions (see "Focal Length and Zoom") and a LCD window with various automatic data displays. The Program Flash 4000 AF is the most powerful in the series of Minolta system flashguns. Its full power referred to ISO 100 and reflector position for 50mm focal length is guide number 40, and it is continuously adjustable down to $^1/_{16}$ of its power even in automatic mode. The reflector can be swung through 90° upwards and also to the right and left for indirect flash illumination (bounce). Further facilities are: AF metering flash (see also "Light for AF"), flash-ready indicator, answer-back signal for sufficient exposure, etc.

The Program Flash 4000 AF requires four batteries for its power supply, either alkaline or rechargeable batteries, size AA, or LR6. Don't use mixed sets of batteries or some fresh and some partially exhausted batteries (see "Battery Care" in the chapter "Camera Care"). The battery compartment is at the side of the unit. Move the grooved sliding cover to reveal the compartment, insert four AA-size batteries according to the markings for correct polarity and replace cover.

Push the flashgun FULLY into the accessory shoe. All ancillary contacts must make full contact in the accessory shoe, otherwise the control functions cannot be activated. Secure by the knurled locking screw. Move main switch from OFF to ON. A low whistling sound will be audible which ceases after a few seconds and the red flash symbol illuminates, indicating that the flash is ready. The selected output level is shown in the top line of the LCD data field, the middle line shows the focal length position of the zoom reflector, which moves automatically into the correct position (see "Focal Length and Zoom") and the bottom line shows whether TTL or manual was chosen, also the distance range for which the flash will supply sufficient output. The latter display appears only if the camera is switched on and the release has been lightly depressed. The distance range display disappears as soon as the metering circuit switches off after the usual 10 seconds. The other LCD values remain.

The flashgun will switch off automatically 15 minutes after it reaches the "flash ready" state or after the last time the camera release has been touched. If the main switch is kept to ON, then the flashgun will reactivate as soon as the release is depressed again.

Should it be difficult to read the LCD on the data screen because of poor light, then the data field display may be illuminated by switching on the LIGHT key. The light is extinguished automatically after 8 seconds.

Choice of Power Output and Flash Range

There are a total of six selectable output levels available on the Program Flash 4000 AF, indicated as MD $^1/_{16}$, $^1/_8$, $^1/_4$, $^1/_2$ and FULL in the top line of the LCD field. The selected level is shown in brackets, i.e. (FULL) for full output. Depressing the grey key on the right marked LEVEL will move the brackets to the next lower level, i.e. from (FULL) to ($^1/_2$), to ($^1/_4$) and so on and then from (MD) back to (FULL). The MD-level corresponds to about 4% of the full output; in this setting it is important to choose a flashing rate of less than 0.5

second with rechargeable batteries to allow motorized continuous shooting (see "Flash Photography with Motor Drive" in the chapter "Motor Drive and Control Functions").

In all shooting modes except in MANUAL the lower line in the data field displays TTL (see "Manual Flash") and the distance range, for example 0.7-8m. There is a small switch top left of the data field by which the distance reading may be changed to feet -ft-. The displayed distance range depends on a combination of selected or automatically chosen values: film speed, power level, zoom reflector position, diffuser disc on/off, perhaps also preselected aperture value. The microprocessor within the Program Flash 4000 AF calculates from these parameters the resulting distance range and displays the result. The flash will almost always supply the correct amount of illumination for the shot; the photographer need not worry about anything else.

The lowest limit of the setting range lies at 0.7m in the close distance range. Using combinations of low output level, small aperture and low ISO values it may be possible that only 0.7m, together with an arrow pointing left (= distance limit below 0.7m), appears. In this case a higher output level and a larger aperture should be selected, perhaps by changing the shooting mode. For long distance settings the 28m upper limit, together with an arrow pointing to the right, will appear.

The red flash symbol flashes slowly in the viewfinder when the setup is ready. This is different from the continuous light showing flash-ready at the back of the Program Flash 4000 AF. After the shot has been taken, a rapid flashing of the same LED symbol indicates that sufficient illumination was available for that shot. Above the legend EXP on the flashgun the green OK illuminates at the same time.

Under exceptional circumstances it may happen that a

subject positioned within the indicated distance range may be underexposed. The limit values indicated on the flash assume a certain level of ambient lighting, mainly due to reflected flashlight from walls, ceiling, etc. When taking flash photographs in very large rooms, or at night outside, such additional light will not be available and the effective far limit will be shorter. However, in these situations the answer-back signal will also report correct exposure.

The flashing rate, that is the time when the flash is ready for the next shot, depends on the selected output level and also on the output of the previous flash. The lower the output level the quicker the flashgun will be ready for the next shot because recharging requirements are lower.

Focal Length and Zoom

The zoom reflector of the Program Flash 4000 AF has four adjustable positions that adapt the flash beam to the viewing angle of the lens. The horizontal illumination angle covers 70° when the reflector is completely pushed in; the subsequent positions illuminate angles of 60°, 46° and 36°. These angles correspond to lens focal lengths of 28mm, 35mm, 50mm and 70mm. These values also appear, when the camera is switched on, in the middle line for focal lengths in the data screen of the flashgun. To be precise, these angles are a little larger than the viewing angles of the appropriate lens: a certain decrease in light intensity is allowed for in the limits of the illumination angle, and this tolerance should produce even illumination of the image field. The vertical illumination angles are stated by Minolta to be 53°, 45°, 34° and 26° again with additional allowance for decrease of light.

The zoom reflector may be controlled automatically or manually, in both instances by motor drive. In Automatic mode the appropriate lens focal length of the lens, or the focal length selected on the zoom together with AUTO ZOOM, will appear in the focal length field. If the lens is changed or the lens focal length is adjusted, then the zoom reflector adjusts automatically to accommodate the selected viewing angle that is also displayed in the data field. The adjustment is by steps, without intermediate values, always at the 70 - 50 - 35 - 28mm focal lengths. For the longer focal lengths the reflector and display are set to 70mm. If a 24mm wide-angle lens is attached, then only "≗" will be displayed instead of the focal length.

Depressing the zoom key (second grey key from the left at the rear of the flashgun) will change the display from AUTO ZOOM to MANUAL ZOOM, the reflector will move to position 28mm, if it is not already at this setting, and this focal length indication will appear in the data field. Depressing the zoom key again will move the reflector to the next position, 35mm, and the display will change accordingly; depressing again will adjust to 50mm and then to 70mm, the next time the position will be AUTO ZOOM. The reflector can only be adjusted by motor drive.

The zoom control acts in similar fashion with the reflector swinging to the top or sideways. In AUTO ZOOM the reflector will move only if the camera is also switched on; in MANUAL ZOOM it is possible also if the camera is not switched on, provided the flashgun is ON.

The automatic distance range in the lower section of the data field changes together with the reflector adjustment; the reflector angle is one of the parameters determining the light output and therefore the illumination range. The wide-angle diffuser spreads the flashlight further sideways, but this at the cost of the directly projected intensity, which decreases to half the previous value. The illumination depth indication adjusts immediately and PANEL is displayed simultaneously in the data field. In zoom position 28mm, or with an 24mm lens attached to the camera and the wide-angle diffuser, the illuminated image angle corresponds to the viewing angle of the 24mm lens (ca $53° \times 74°$).

Flash in Program Mode

Now the program modes: the simplest to use is the Program or P-function. Set the shooting mode selector on the camera to PROGRAM, switch flashgun on and release as soon as the flash-ready symbol appears. That's it. The only function you could perform is to check the previously mentioned answer-back signal, OK at the flashgun and rapidly flashing flash symbol in the viewfinder which indicates that the exposure was correct. The distance range indication may vary a little, as the aperture selected by the program mode changes and the metering cell in the camera senses lighter or darker subject areas.

Program shift is inoperative when using flash in program mode: activating the shutter speed and aperture keys do not affect the programmed settings.

Preselection Mode

Using aperture priority (function mode A on the shooting mode selector) allows you to control the exposure. At this setting the flashgun will set the shutter speed to $1/250$ second (flash synchronization time) as soon as "flash-ready" state is obtained. The aperture may now be selected, provided the subject is still within the displayed flash range. In this mode it is therefore possible to obtain the greatest possible depth of field by choosing the smallest possible aperture, or to cover a deep spatial distance by using a larger aperture. The distance range display continuously adjusts in the data field of the

Program Flash 4000 AF and the answer-back signal reports after the shot whether the exposure and the flash output were correct. As usual in A-mode, the selected aperture value appears in the data field on top of the camera and in the viewfinder.

The second possibility in preselection function is the S-mode (shutter speed priority). After the flash-ready signal is given the aperture is automatically set to f/5.6 and the corresponding distance range appears in the data field. The range depends, as previously, on the film speed and the zoom reflector position, but no longer on the metered subject luminance because the aperture is now fixed. The automatic exposure control measures the flash by TTL-metering.

In this shooting mode it is possible to preselect a shutter speed between $1/250$ second and 30 seconds. Shutter speeds shorter than $1/250$ second will automatically be adjusted to $1/250$ second after flash-ready. The selected time has no influence on the flash exposure, but it affects the exposure of the naturally illuminated surroundings. For shutter speeds close to $1/250$ second the final effect corresponds more or less to that achieved in aperture priority mode (A-function). For the longer exposure times the surrounding details will be shown more pronounced, and may even overwhelm the subject that had been illuminated by the flash.

For slow shutter speeds care has to be taken that the picture will not be blurred due to camera shake. Even the sharply reproduced flashed subject could be super-imposed by unsharp images exposed by available light.

The shooting procedure is the same as previously: switch flashgun on, and touch camera release, wait for "flash-ready" signal and check if the displayed distance range is sufficient for the subject. If the subject lies outside the distance range then it may be necessary to switch to A-function in order to change to a larger aperture.

Fill-in Flash

If the surroundings are lighter, or the shutter speed relatively long, then the flash is mainly used to fill-in dark areas. Using normal flash intensity would probably overexpose the main subject under these circumstances.

The AEL-key has been provided for this situation. First set the camera to S-mode (shutter speed priority), select shutter speed, switch flashgun on and set the distance by autofocus. Depress the grey AEL-key and keep depressed. This will adjust the aperture from f/5.6 to the correct exposure for the surroundings.

Still keeping the AEL-key depressed, check the distance range; the subject has to be within the indicated range. Please note that if the surroundings are bright or a longer shutter speed has been chosen, then the aperture will get smaller after the AEL-key has been depressed, causing the far limit of the distance range to be reduced. If the light is poor or the chosen shutter speed short, then the aperture will be larger, increasing the far limit as a result.

Now, still with AEL-key depressed, the release may be depressed. The automatic exposure control adjusts the exposure level to the available lighting conditions and reduces the flash duration to prevent overexposure of the main subject.

In A-function the fill-in flash procedure is less complicated, but also less versatile. Meter the subject with flashgun switched off and adjust the aperture so that the resulting shutter speed value is no shorter than $1/125$ second. This aperture value remains the operative value. Now switch the flashgun on (the shutter speed will now move to $1/250$ second) and depress the AEL-key. This causes the shutter speed setting to move to the next-shortest previously obtained speed. In the above example this will be $1/125$ second. Check the distance range and release: the answer-back signal will report correct exposure. Using this method the final result will not look like a harshly illuminated flash image, and the background will be shown to better effect.

Fill-in flash is often used to fill-in dark shadows in daylight; in particular in very bright backlit shots, i.e. whenever there are excessive contrasts. Here too the flash should not be too strong to dominate the daylight. Together with the Program Flash 4000 AF the Minolta 9000 manages this almost entirely on its own: because of TTL metering the camera reduces the flash duration in bright ambient light to fill-in effect and in darker situations the flash is again the main source of illumination.

Manual Flash

In the shooting modes described above, the flash duration is controlled by TTL metering. In manual operation (functions selector to MANUAL) you have the choice between TTL metering and manual flash control.

With TTL metering the flash functions are similar to the S-function. Switch flashgun on, select aperture and shutter speed values (speed not shorter than $^1/_{250}$ second) by adjusting to the displayed values in the viewfinder, so that either +0 or −0 appears next to the "M" in the viewfinder. Check that the important subject detail lies within the distance range displayed in the data field and release. If necessary the distance range can be extended by choosing a larger aperture with faster shutter speed. The answer-back signal reports sufficient exposure by TTL-controlled flash.

To use the flash in fully manual mode you depress the TTL/M-key at the rear of the Program Flash 4000 AF (second grey key from the right). Instead of "TTL", "M" will be displayed in the bottom line of the data field and only the distance range. The flashgun will now deliver exactly the set output as the TTL control is inoperative.

The exposure is determined by the guide number, which simplifies the processor electronics. The correct exposure depends on the correct adjustment of aperture and distance. First you bring the main subject into sharp focus, reading the final value off the display on the lens. This distance has to agree with the distance displayed in the LCD data field of the flashgun. The latter value is adjusted to the distance setting on the lens. This may be done by changing the flash output between $1/16$ and FULL or by adjusting the aperture value. If the two distance settings are in agreement, then the flash exposure will be correct.

Switching the Program Flash 4000 AF from TTL to M is possible only if the function selector on the camera is also set to MANUAL; in all the other settings the TTL/M key is inoperative. When the flash is switched off and on again, the setting will automatically revert to TTL.

Indirect Flash

The tilt and turn reflector on the Program Flash 4000 AF allows the flash to be bounced off the ceiling or a wall. Provided such a surface is close enough and has sufficient reflectivity, this indirect flash will provide soft, uniform illumination of the subject, without the hard shadows that are typical of many a flash photograph. Flash illumination depends to a very large degree on the distance, luminance, etc. of the reflecting surfaces and TTL metering is therefore essential for indirect flash illumination.

Distance range means very little under these circumstances and the distance range indicator disappears from the data field display. A lot of the light output is lost in indirect flashing and so it is therefore best to set the flashgun to FULL output. The best function to use in this case is aperture priority mode (A-function) as the larger apertures are more suitable (the aperture value chosen by the program mode may be too small). Manual mode with TTL metering is also quite suitable.

The ceiling or wall chosen to reflect the flash should have good diffusing qualities as shiny surfaces are less suitable, and be white or at least neutral in colour. Bouncing the flash off highly coloured surfaces will produce a colour cast. Swing the zoom reflector of the Program Flash 4000 AF such that it points as far as possible half way between the subject and the camera toward the wall or the ceiling. The ideal angle lies somewhere between 60° and 90°. The angles are marked at the rear of the reflector and it engages from 45° (from 30° in lateral deflection) in 15° steps.

Indirect flash should only supply indirect light. The zoom position therefore should be set to 50 or 70mm especially for larger distances, because the flash light falling from the zoom reflector directly onto the subject produces very uneven illumination. However, it may be desirable to use indirect flash illumination as fill-in flash (see "Two Flashguns").

To obtain the best aperture value you adjust the reflector as for direct flash and set the aperture to ensure that the subject is within the displayed distance range. Then turn the reflector to indirect flash position and open the aperture by two stops. If, for example, the data field shows a flash illumination range of 6m at aperture setting f/5.6 then the correct aperture setting will be f/2.8 for indirect flash, provided the lens is fast enough. After the shot has been taken the camera will report back on whether the illumination was sufficient. It is therefore important to check the OK signal on the flashgun or the rapidly flashing symbol in the viewfinder. In the event that no confirmation appears, the shot has to be repeated with a larger aperture or at a closer distance setting.

It is not always possible to find a suitable surface to reflect the flash. In this case Bounce Reflector II will provide sufficiently diffuse illumination. The 28x40cm trapezoid screen is attached to the upward pointing zoom reflector so that it reflects the flash light forward onto the subject. It produces a soft direct light which isn't quite as diffuse as the indirect illumination bounced off the ceiling, but for some subjects this is the ideal illumination.

Setting-up: Open the Bounce Reflector II and secure by turning the locking ring. Insert the 12cm long bar on the shaft of the screen angled at 45° and push the other end of the bar into the diffuser adapter. The diffuser adapter looks like the wide-angle diffuser, but it is fully transparent and has a fixing device for the shaft. There are another two smaller adapters available for different Minolta flashguns.

Swing the zoom reflector of the Program Flash 4000 AF fully forward with flashgun ·attached to camera and set it manually to the 28mm position (the zoom reflector is fully pushed home). Attach the diffuser screen with adapter on the zoom reflector so that the screen sits at an angle of 45° pointing forward. The equipment is now ready and may be used like a normal forward illuminating flash. The distance range may again be checked as for a normally forward pointing zoom reflector, deducting 40% from the displayed value. If the 4000 AF indicates 10m as the illuminated distance, the effective range with indirect flash and diffuser screen will be 6m.

The zoom reflector will normally point straight up (90°) when used with the Bounce Reflector II. For close-ups the parallax effect may be reduced by swinging the zoom reflector to the 75° position, in the extreme close range (e.g. 1:1 reproduction scale with the 50mm macro lens)

158

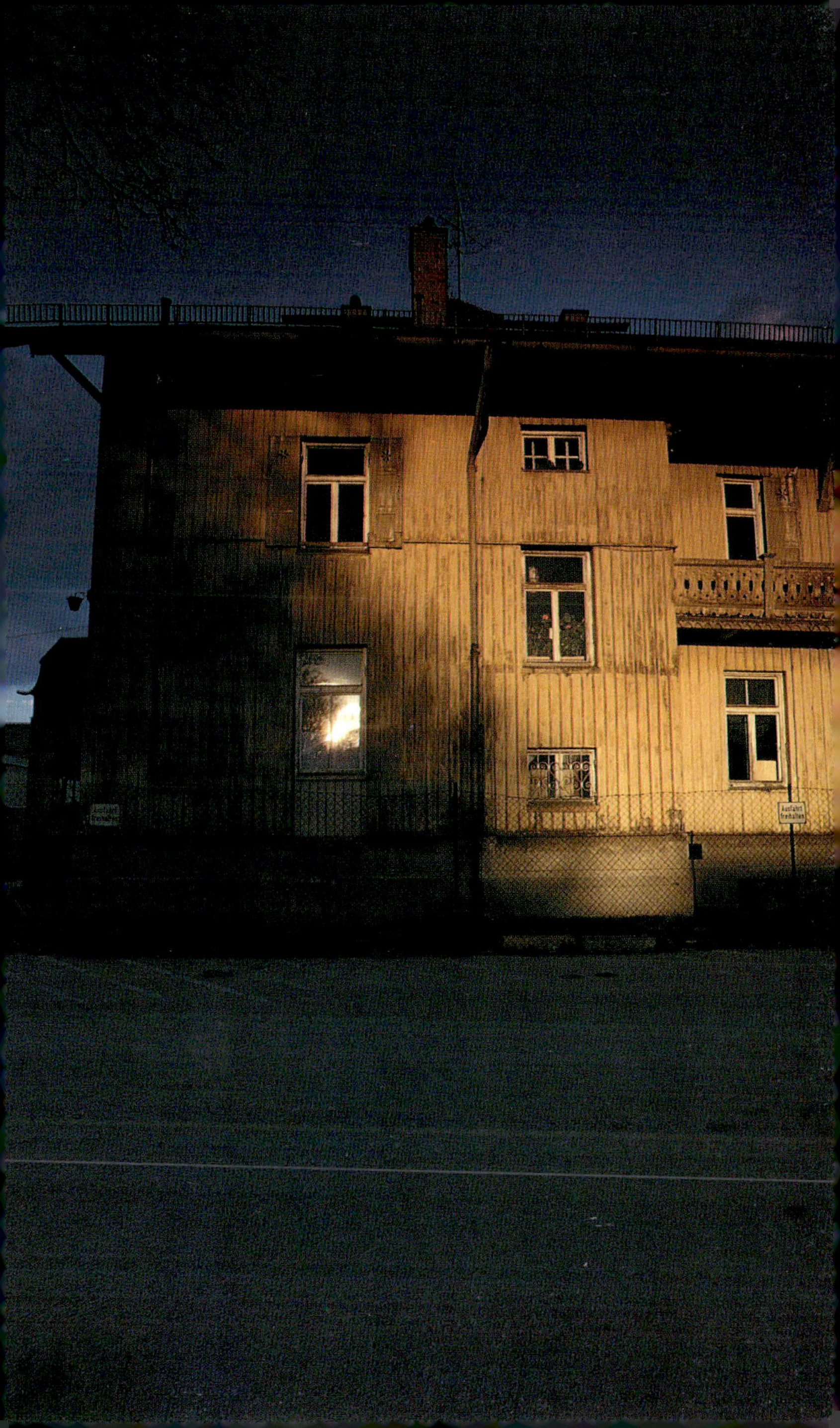

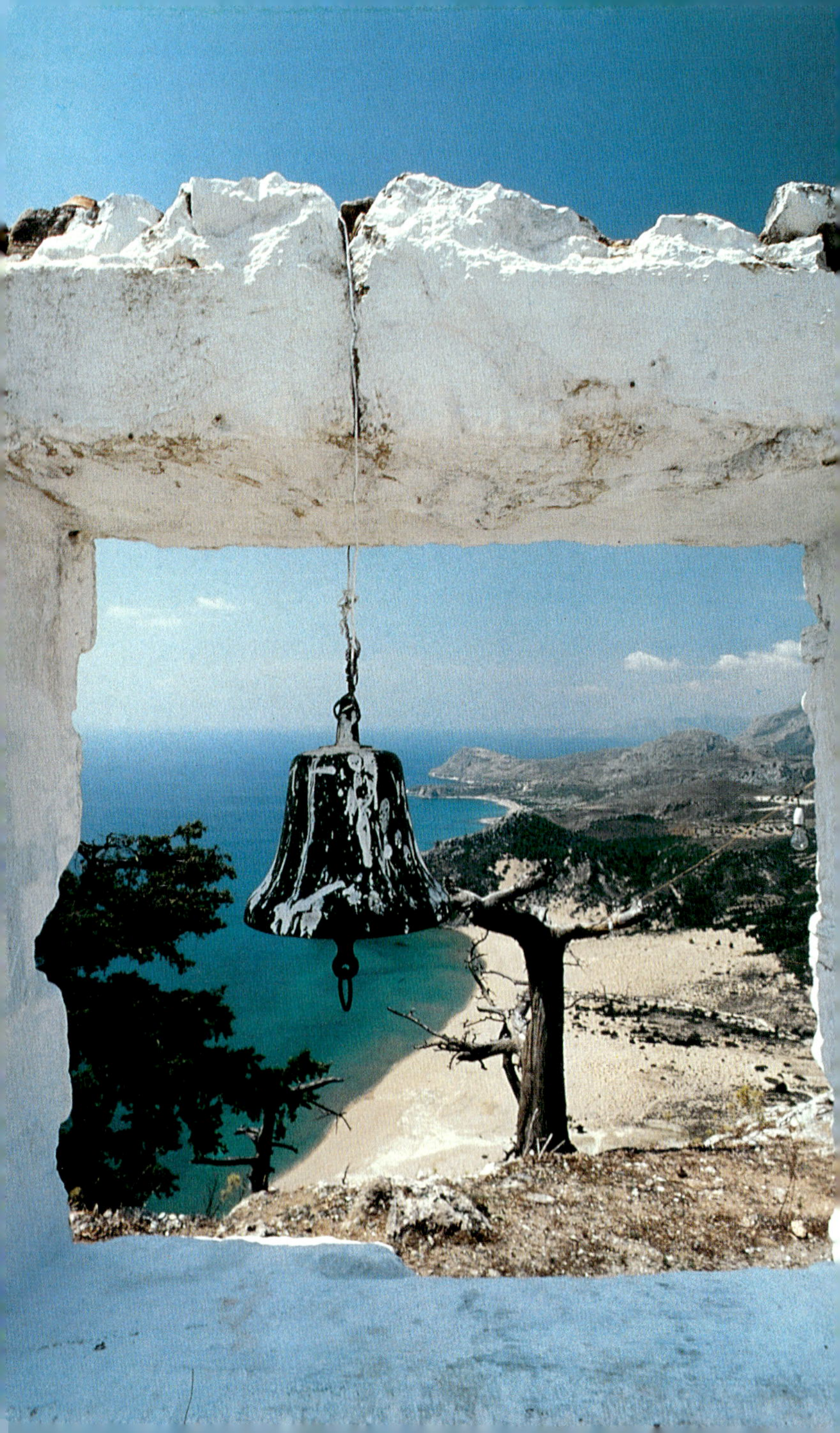

even to 60°. This arrangement is ideal for still-life in the close-up range as it provides practically shadow-free illumination. It may also be possible to work with the flash set at a reduced output.

Always check the answer-back signal after each frame; if no signal is given then the shot has to be repeated, either with a larger aperture or increased flash output.

To store away, remove screen from adapter. Return shaft to 90° position, release strut by turning the locking ring and store folded screen in its case (the adapter can also be accommodated there).

Program Flash 2800 AF

This compact flash unit, together with batteries it weighs just under half as much as the 4000 AF, produces a little more than half the output of the 4000 AF (max. guide number 28). It is less sophisticated than its powerful brother but offers similar TTL facilities. The 2800 AF has neither a zoom reflector nor can it be inclined for indirect flash. The illumination angle corresponds to a 35mm lens which may be adapted down to 28mm with a wide-angle diffuser. This flashgun has a display slide switch instead of the LCD panel and only two selectable output levels and is solely controlled by TTL metering.

Just like the 4000 AF this flashgun is also powered by four alkaline or rechargeable batteries. The battery compartment is on the side of the unit. Push slide cover to the top and insert batteries, taking care to follow polarity as indicated inside, and close cover. The film speed may be selected by slide switch at the rear of the flashgun (range ISO 25 to 1000). This switch will automatically adjust the mechanical display of distance

---

Freshly whitewashed walls in the bright Greek sunlight required particularly careful exposure.   *Photo: Jürgen Lehr*

ranges. The TTL control depends, as previously, on the film speed selection on the camera.

The blue bars on the distance range display indicate distance ranges at full power (Hi/Lo switch on the left not depressed), the blue/white hatched bars indicate distances for 1/16 output (Hi/Lo switch depressed). The flashing rate with rechargeable batteries is reduced to a maximum of 0.4 seconds at the latter setting, it is therefore possible to take serial shots of up to 2 frames per second.

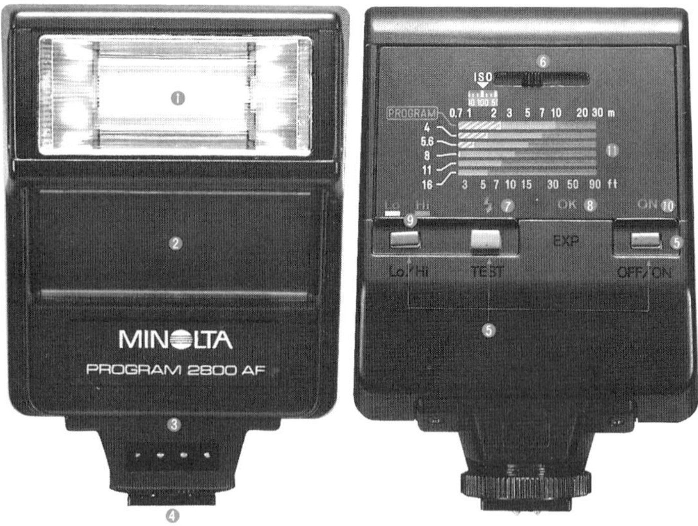

The smaller of the two special flashguns, the program Flash 2800 AF. The reflector for the infra-red metering flash (2) is just below the normal reflector. The metering flash projects a small red pattern on the subject which is used by the AF facility to focus in the dark. A plug allows an outside power supply, thus increasing flashing rate and reducing intervals between the flashes. The contacts are in the plug (4), providing the connections to the camera. The flashgun is operated by the following keys: main switch (5 – right), test key to release a test flash (5 – centre) and selector key (5 – left) for long distance (H) or fast flashing rate (Lo). The display shows if the flashgun is switched on (10), what output level had been selected (9), whether flash is ready (7) and that the flash illumination was sufficient (7). The film speed slide switch (6) affects only the range scale (11), the ISO value is directly supplied by the camera.

The top bar refers to program mode, the others to selected apertures between f/4 to f/16. Larger and smaller apertures are also possible, only there is not enough space for more bars. Values outside the indicated range may be calculated by doubling the distance range for an increase by two aperture stops. For example, if the distance limit is given as 7m for aperture f/5.6, then the distance would be doubled to 14m for f/2.8, with aperture f/1.4 this would even be 28m. Similarly a limit of 10m and aperture f/4 would increase to 20m when the aperture is opened to f/2.

Using the diffuser, the distance is reduced to the next smaller aperture opening, e.g. using aperture f/4 the limit will be reduced from 10m to 7m, as for aperture f/5.6 without diffuser.

To switch on, the ON/OFF key is depressed; the display ON will illuminate. Depressing this key again will switch the flashgun off. The unit will also automatically switch off, like the 4000 AF. The flash symbol (red) and "OK" symbol (green) report correct exposure and flash-ready, as described for the 4000 AF.

In Program Mode (camera shooting mode selector to PROGRAM) the Minolta 9000 will select a shutter speed between $^1/_{250}$ and $^1/_{60}$ second, the subject should lie within the distance range indicated by the PROGRAM bar. In bright conditions the flash duration will be reduced (fill-in flash).

With Aperture Preselection (A-function) the distance range indicated by the bar markers on the 2800 AF apply for the various aperture values (the PROGRAM range also for aperture f/2.8).

With Shutter Speed Preselection (S-function) the camera will select aperture f/5.6 after the "flash-ready" signal has been received and it is then possible to choose any shutter speed setting down to $^1/_{250}$ second. The fill-in flash and long exposure mode (with AEL-key) will function in both the A-function and S-function.

In Manual Mode (shooting mode selector to MANUAL). TTL metering functions in this mode; you select any suitable aperture/shutter speed combination. When the camera receives the "flash-ready" signal it automatically selects $^1/_{250}$ second as flash synchronization time if a shorter time had been chosen manually. It is not possible to change to M (without TTL) with this flashgun.

Program Flash 1800 AF

This is the smallest flashgun in the AF series. It has the same facilities as models 4000 AF and 2800 AF, but only one output level and no distance range indication. Its guide number is 18 (ISO 100). The illumination angle is equivalent to 35mm and with wide-angle diffuser it may be used with a 28mm lens. In the latter case the guide number is reduced to 14. The range of this flashgun is therefore rather limited. The 1800 AF is mainly useful for intimate situations. Its advantage lies in its compact, light construction (it weighs about 170 g) and the fact it will fit easily into a pocket.

Distance ranges for film speeds ISO 100 and ISO 400 are marked at the instrument back for program mode. The instrument range has to be calculated for the other shooting modes by dividing the guide number by the aperture value displayed in the viewfinder. The usual flash-ready symbols appear on the flashgun and in the viewfinder (red flash symbol); the answer-back for correct exposure is provided by fast flashing of the flash symbol in the viewfinder. Manual flash release is not provided.

The 1800 AF requires 4 size AAA batteries (or LR03,

Mn 2400, etc.) or one lithium 6V battery, at the moment only by Duracell DL 223A or National Panasonic BRP2P; the similar looking Sanyo 2CR5 does not fit!. This new type of battery gives twice the number of flashes as compared with the alkaline batteries and a faster flashing rate of only $2^1/_2$ seconds. With rechargeable batteries the flashing rate is a reasonable 3 seconds, but the capacity is considerably lower.

The size AAA batteries are inserted as usual into the battery compartment. The lithium battery, if used, will move a sliding cover for the AAA batteries aside, revealing two alternative contacts for connection. Another advantage of lithium batteries is that they can be stored for very long periods with practically no loss in capacity.

Light for AF

The program flash units in the AF-series supply illumination not only for the subject, but also for the focusing facility. These are metering flashes that are emitted when the flashgun is fully charged as shown by the flash-ready indicator at the back of the instrument.

In poor lighting conditions, when flash is normally used, the double arrow points are illuminated indicating that the AF facility cannot function when the release and autofocus button is lightly depressed. If the flashgun is attached and ready to use and the release is lightly touched, then the flashgun will emit one or several short metering flashes which are used by the AF system to focus. Each metering flash, to be precise a light impulse sent by a small lamp behind a red filter, has a duration of $^1/_2$ second. If this is insufficient for the AF system to focus, then a second impulse is sent. That will be sufficient and the green circular diode lights up in the viewfinder to indicate that the camera is set. The metering result is automatically stored.

The red metering flashes are just visible in front of the camera. They may be seen more clearly only if you are situated exactly within the target area. Light concentrating reflectors direct the metering flashes onto a subject area corresponding to that of the target field. The left reflector directs the beam to the more distant subject area, the right one to the closer range up to 2.5m.

Using the metering flash it is possible to focus on subjects between about 1m and 7m (Program Flash 4000 AF) or to 5m (2800 AF) and to 4.5m (the 1800 AF has only one metering lamp). The close-up range is determined by the flash parallax as at the shorter distances even the left metering flash is not able to illuminate the subject area within the metering field. The far limit of the metering flash does not necessarily correspond to the illumination range of the flashgun.

Minolta state the above specifications for the 50mm standard lens. However, these apply also to other focal lengths; to zooms, but for focal lengths in excess of 135mm they are less reliable. Firstly because it is rather difficult to maintain correct focusing position in the dark and secondly, as it is easy to exceed the metering limit with a longer lens.

In the 4000 AF, the metering flash is housed in the battery chamber. In this model the metering flash is always pointed forward, even if the reflector is in a different position.

Control Grip CG-1000

The flashgun mounted directly on the camera will provide flat front lighting. This will cause rather heavy shadows directly behind the subject which could be rather irritating. Apart from using indirect flash there is another way of directing the light. This is achieved by placing the

166

flashgun laterally and above the camera by the use of the so-called Control Grip CG-1000. This consists of a camera bracket, a grip with battery compartment, an extension cable, and one of the AF-flashguns. The batteries are loaded into the compartment and are used to augment the set in the flashgun itself, thus increasing the flashing rate and flash capacity.

Move the sliding cover away from the compartment and remove battery retainer. Insert 6 size AA batteries, the same as for flashguns 4000 AF and 2800 AF, observing polarity, and insert retainer in compartment and close the sliding cover. Thanks to guides and rivets, the retainer will only fit one way.

Instead of this battery retainer it is also possible to fit a rechargeable battery pack NP-2 into the grip. This may be recharged with recharger QC-1.

Push flashgun 4000 AF or 2800 AF, but not the 1800 AF, into the accessory shoe on top of the grip. There need not be any batteries in the flashgun itself, as the power supply is provided by the batteries in the grip. But

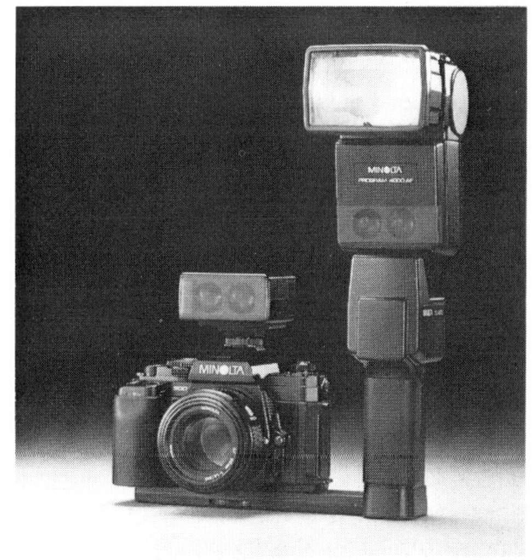

An excellent equipment combination: Motor Drive MD-90, Control Grip, Program Flash 4000 AF and the AF Illumination Unit, facilitating series shots with flash illumination for up to 5 frames per second.

the arrangement cannot function if there are no batteries in the grip. On the other hand the automatic setting of the zoom reflector will be inoperative if there are no batteries in the flashgun; only the focal length indication will blink in the data field.

Screw camera bracket to bottom of camera and ensure that the four pin contacts and the thicker blank locating pin engage in the Minolta 9000. Fully push home the plug end of the camera bracket into the bracket opening underneath on the grip side. The electrical connection to the camera is now via the plug contacts in the grip, in the bracket and in the camera base.

This sequence of assembling flashgun on flash, bracket on camera, then the bracket onto the grip is the easiest, in particular as the bracket on its own is much easier to fix to the camera than when the grip is already attached.

Apart from the AF metering flash, for which the AF-Illuminator Unit is required, all other flash modes are fully functional, just as for the flashguns 4000 AF and 2800 AF mounted directly into the accessory shoe. A rectangular red diode is illuminated by touching the release as long as the camera's metering facility is switched on.

Flash off the Leash

Mounted on the grip the flash is set about 11cm to the left as seen from behind, and 4.5cm above the top of the camera. This makes quite a difference in beaming the light and reduces the risk of the so-called "red eye effect"; red dots instead of pupils in the eyes of people and animal portraits.

The lighting effect is even better if the flash is even further away from the camera and connected via the extension cable. To effect this, remove the bracket from the grip, depress the little grey key at the rear of the

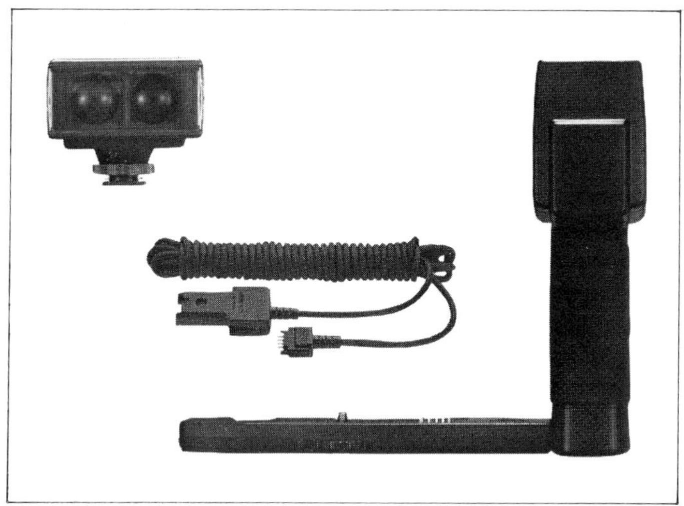

A wide range of applications is opened up: the Program Flash 4000 AF, with the 2800 AF and Control Grip CG-1000. Also part of the equipment: the AF-Illumination Unit AI-1000, Extension Cable EC-1000 and Control Grip CG-1000.

grip and pull the track out of the grip at the same time, and push the large plug of the cable, with tripod thread pointing down, into the grip until it engages. Now connect the small plug to the free end of the bracket. The latter plug can only be connected the correct way; it has a round and a square locating pin that fit into the appropriate holes in the track.

The flash can now be placed anywhere up to 5m away from the camera to provide lateral, top or low light. It is safer to mount the flashgun and grip on a tripod (tripod thread underneath the large plug). The TTL metering cell in the Minolta 9000 will now control the flash duration, in all shooting modes, according to the available light, e.g. in S-function for slower shutter speeds.

Two Flashguns

Attaching the flashgun via the Control Grip CG-1000

means that the accessory shoe on the camera is free. Using two flashguns provides better, and more controllable illumination. The flash on the grip will provide the main illumination, the flash on the camera the fill-in. The TTL-metering will control both flashguns for correct exposure. There are two modes of control using the ratio-switch at the left side of the grip.

If this switch is set to OFF, then the electronic control will distribute the output equally between the two flashguns, provided they are the same models. The relative effect on the picture will depend on the distance from the subject of each of the flash units. The illumination effect of a flashgun at 6m distance is naturally different from one that is only 4m away.

If the ratio switch is set to ON, then the control circuit will allow $^2/_3$ of the power output to go to the main flash in the grip and $^1/_3$ to the one in the camera's accessory shoe. This difference in illumination takes effect when both flashguns are placed at equal distances from the subject. If the flashguns are at different distances from the subject with the main flash closer to the subject, then the difference in illumination will be even more pronounced.

To determine the correct distance ranges is a little more difficult with two flash units. It is therefore most important to check the signal after the shot has been taken and repeat it with a larger aperture and/or shorter flash distance. If the models used are different (i.e. the 4000 AF in the grip and the 2800 AF or the 1800 AF on the camera) then the control circuit will distribute the flash output proportionally to the maximum output of each flashgun.

Three or even more flashguns may be connected via CD cable and Triple Connector to the 4000 AF or, with an accessory shoe, to the 2800 AF. In this case the flashguns can be controlled partly via the grip and partly via the accessory shoe. The ratio switch will distribute the output, as previously described between the two connections.

A third non-system flashgun can further be connected at the rear of the CG-1000, but this will not be controlled by the TTL-metering cell. This connection is provided for independent auxiliary light (e.g. background lighting). Such a flashgun can only be triggered if there is a flashgun in flash-ready state in the grip.

The AF Flash Illuminator

The AF-metering flash of AF flashguns can be pointed at the subject only if the flashgun is actually mounted on the camera. If the flashgun is mounted on the CG-1000, and no second flash is on the camera, then it is necessary to use the AF-Illuminator Unit that it part of the CG-1000. It looks like a small flash unit, but contains only the two metering lights as normally incorporated in the 4000 AF and the 2800 AF.

To use it, insert four small batteries (size AAA, or LR03 – rechargeable batteries are not suitable), observing correct polarity, in the battery compartment and fit the device into the accessory shoe. This illuminator will work in exactly the same manner as the metering flash in the flashgun (see "light for AF") provided the control grip is connected to the camera and the flashgun is attached and in flash-ready state. It covers a range of about 1m to 7m.

Remote Controlled Metering

With the Minolta Flash Meter IV and Data Receiver DR-1000 you can explore professional flash arrangements in studio lighting with more elaborate equipment. Flash Meter IV will meter flash illumination for different illumination combinations of several studio units and will take into account the permanent available light. Metering can be performed in various metering and operational modes (subject or light metering, with aperture pre-selection,etc.), LCD displays on the meter show not only the measured values but also film speed, type of metering, shutter speed and additional multiflash units, if required. This meter can also analyse and store the metered values.

A special function combines these applications with the Minolta 9000: that is data transfer by infra-red signals from the flash meter to the receiver mounted on the camera. The latter is attached to the camera's accessory shoe and is connected on the one hand to the remote control release of the camera and on the other to the synchronization or firing circuit of the flash system.

Flash Meter IV meters the appropriate values of the ambient light or combinations under consideration and triggers the flash system. Switching over to send, the data receiver transfers the metered values to the camera (aperture, shutter speed in manual function) and finally triggers the camera's release. The receiver range, powered by a 9V battery, is 7m, sufficient for a studio environment.

Motor Drive and Control Functions

The motorized SLR camera is a development that arose from the professional sports photographers' requirements to capture series of complicated movements by a fast sequence of frames. Modern SLR cameras, almost without exception, are fitted with either an integrated transport motor or at least coupling elements to attach an auxiliary unit. Both these alternatives have their particular advantages and disadvantages. Minolta decided to produce their two less sophisticated models in the AF series, the 5000 and the 7000 with integrated motor. The 9000, being aimed at the professional, has been fitted with contacts for attaching a separate motor unit.

Why? From an engineering point of view the integrated motor, in fact several small motors, is the better solution. They may be employed to use their power exactly where they are needed. It is a better solution than the external motor drive which requires more complicated and not always straightforward power transmissions. This applies in particular to the slower frame sequences (about 2 frames per second) which can be handled quite easily by the lighter motor drives. Moreover, they are easily accommodated within the camera body, such as is the case with the 5000 and the 7000. Convenience of handling, automatic film transport after every frame, and motorized rewinding were more important considerations for these models, than rapid frame sequences.

The priorities for the Minolta 9000, designed with the professional photographer in mind, were somewhat different. The professional sports photographer requires at least 4-5 frames per second and this requires a heavier motor which, in turn, requires more space and is considerably heavier, not only by its own weight, but because the construction of the camera body has to be sturdier to accomodate the heavier unit. The Minolta 9000 is an all-metal construction, the 5000 and the 7000 are of composite construction – metal and plastic. The 9000's faster shutter of $1/4000$ second requires also more motor power than the lighter $1/2000$ second shutters of both the 5000 and the 7000.

It is better to construct a more versatile and powerful but separate motor drive for the professional. The camera itself will not be excessively heavy, although the Minolta 9000 weighs more than both the 7000 and the 5000 which have an integrated motor drive, and one can leave the motor and the battery unit at home if it is not required. Carrying the whole lot puts a considerable strain on your biceps: the motor with recharger weighs 580g, the battery unit 770g, together more than the camera body of the Minolta 9000. With motor attached the camera increases in size by 49mm or 66mm. And what do you get in return?

Motor Drive MD-90

The assembled equipment; 9000 with motor drive MD-90 forms a balanced unit that will be perfectly balanced with either a standard lens or a wide-angle lens. The motor housing connects perfectly with the camera body, forming a smooth uniform shape with the camera grip that sits comfortably in your hands, despite the weight.

The operating elements at the rear are the functions switch to the right, the frame counter, the rewind key and a control lamp for monitoring the functions. Accessible both from the back and the front is the knurled rotating disc for the fixing screw for fixing the motor to the camera. The top of the unit holds the fixing screw, guide pins, contact pins for signal transfer and

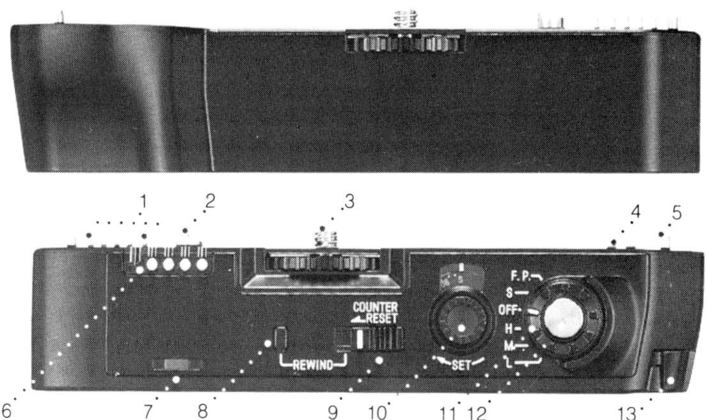

Motor Drive MD-90

1. Contact pins
2. Rewind coupling
3. Fixing screw
4. Film transport coupling
5. Guide pins
6. Contacts for large film magazine
7. Control lamp
8. Rewind knob
9. Frame counter reset
10. Knurled knob for frame counter selector
11. Functions switch
12. Lock for functions selector
13. Battery compartment release

also for flash control when the control grip CG-1000 is attached, and the coupling elements for film transport and rewind. The bottom of the unit carries guide sockets and contacts for the battery unit.

At present there are two energy units available for the motor drive, the BP-90 M for AA size batteries and the NP-90 M with integrated rechargeable batteries. When the motor is attached the circuit is connected via the two-pole round socket beneath the handgrip side. The socket could also connect an external 18VDC power supply. This is not available now, but I am sure Minolta will include one in their catalogue sooner or later.

Energy Unit BP-90M

This container with contacts and connectors accommodates a battery set of twelve size AA batteries, the same types as for the Minolta 9000. Alkaline batteries are the preferred choice, but normal carbon-zinc batteries will do and in case of emergencies even re-chargeable ones, although Minolta advise against these.

To load the batteries; move the slide switch at the bottom of the unit in the direction of the arrow and pull the sprung battery holder fully out. Load the batteries into their compartments, taking care to observe the correct polarity which is marked in the individual compartments. You should remember that the negative pole must always be taken to the sprung contact with the minus sign. The loaded insert is now pushed into the container until it engages; it can only be pushed in in one direction, white dot to white dot.

The test lamp above the little grey button at the back on the right should light up green (17 V or more) if the batteries are fully charged. If the lamp lights up red, then this means that the batteries are partially discharged and if the voltage drops below 16.3V then the lamp does not light up at all and the batteries should be replaced as soon as possible. The drive will still function at a battery voltage of 15V, in particular if rechargeable batteries are loaded, so there is no need to panic if you have no batteries at the ready.

The unit could also be loaded with rechargeable batteries. However, because of their lower initial voltage (1.22 instead of 1.5V) the test display will show

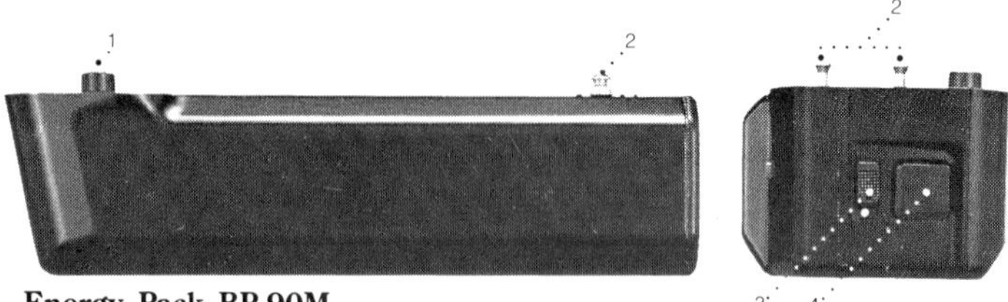

Energy Pack BP-90M

1. Current contacts
2. Installation pins
3. Release switch
4. Battery compartment opener

176

insufficient charge even when they are fully charged and it is possible to find that they are suddenly exhausted right in the middle of a shooting sequence (the motor simply stops). The same also applies to the rechargeable set NP-90M.

A set of fresh alkaline batteries should last for about 50 36-exposure films, according to Minolta. From a set of freshly charged rechargeable batteries you could expect about 35 to 40 films. However, rechargeable batteries need to be regularly recharged, which is not always very convenient. In that case the BP-90N unit is more convenient, and lighter, than rechargeable batteries in the BP-90M unit, and they are the only power source that will achieve up to 5 frames per second.

Energy Unit NP-90M

The NP-90M with its set of 14 rechargeable batteries is only half the height and little more than half the weight of the fully loaded BP-90M. The fully charged set should last about 30 to 35 films according to Minolta, then it will have to be recharged with the charger that is supplied with the unit. Recharging time is about 8 hours.

These statements refer to the unit in constant use. If the unit is not used you should expect it to loose about 1-2 % of its charge daily. After a longer break of days or weeks the unit should be recharged before use. If you need a larger capacity at any one point you would be better advised to use the BP-90M and to take a spare set of batteries.

Connecting the unit is the same for both models. First insert the end with the single pin and the contacts, then press the other end close until it fully cngages. If the other end with the double pins is connected first, then you have to take care that the single-pin end also engages fully. Once the right side is engaged it will not

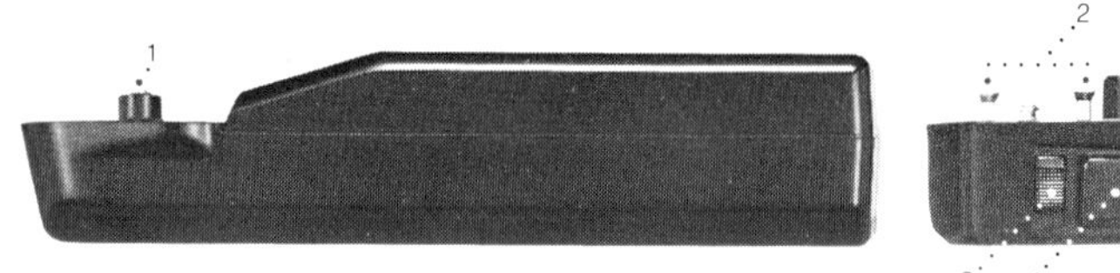

Energy Pack NP-90M

1. Current contacts
2. Installation pins
3. Release switch
4. Battery compartment opener

disengage again after the one on the left has been engaged.

To release, push the release lever at the right rear side of the motor unit in the direction of the arrow and at the same time withdraw the energy unit from this end and then from the other. It is important that the contacts are kept clean. The two separately standing pins form the connection to the second release, the other four serve for signal transfer between the camera and the bracket of the control grip CG-1000. Before the unit is inserted or removed the selector switch should be set to OFF.

Camera Preparation

This is how the MD-90 is connected to the Minolta 9000. Set the functions switch to OFF (press blank button and turn knurled knob), insert guide pin at the right side of the motor drive into the corresponding guide hole and at the same time insert the fixing screw into the tripod thread at the camera base. Now secure the screw by turning the rotating disc. Ensure that there are no foreign particles between the bottom of the camera and the motor unit; the motor has to be in complete contact with the camera.

To remove simply loosen the fixing screw and disengage the motor.

Using the motor simplifies film loading; the motor will

advance the film to the first frame. Set functions switch on the motor to OFF and push COUNTER RESET in the direction of the arrow. The frame counter will reset to S (start). Insert film in the usual manner (see chapter "Camera and Film") and close camera back. Now turn the motor function selector to S and depress camera release. The motor advances the film automatically to the first frame.

The Frame Counter

Unlike the frame counter on the camera, the counter on the MD-90 has an additional function. It displays the number of available frames and switches the motor off as soon as the last frame is spent. To be able to fulfil this function the counter has to be correctly set. As soon as the film is loaded and advanced to the first frame, the counter will show "36". If the loaded film has 36 exposures, then you need not do anything. For shorter films the counter has to be re-set by turning the knurled knob of the frame counter in the direction of the arrow (SET) until the required number appears, e.g. 24. Should you have made an error then you depress COUNTER RESET to display S and repeat the process. This ensures that the motor switches off before the last frame is reached and the perforations are not torn due to excessive force. This could easily happen in cold weather as the film material becomes more brittle.

Even numbers are indicated by white numbers, the intermediate odd numbers by red dots. The numbers "36, 24, 20 and 12, and also S, are shown in red to correspond to the most usual commercially available film lengths. The largest number on the counter is 36. It is possible to expose a 37th or even 38th frame by resetting the counter and carrying on. I don't see much sense in that though, this one or perhaps two frames certainly

The frame counter on the motor drive MD-90 shows the remaining frames. The required number to be shot may be preselected on the knurled knob.

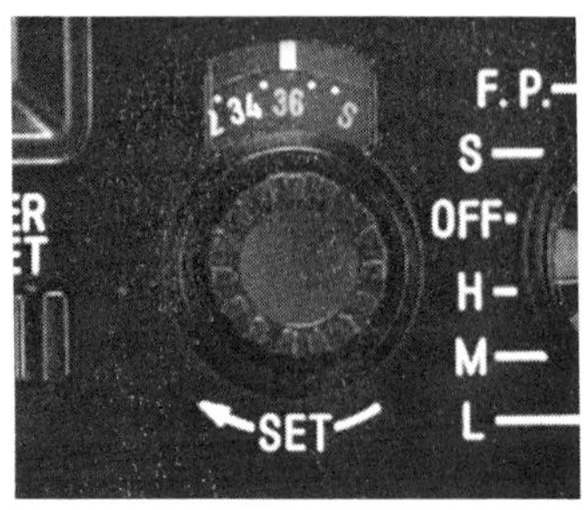

cannot be used in this fashion to present a series. After all, the frame counter and the automatic cut-off is designed to warn you that the film is used up.

It used to be possible to obtain films with 72 frames. In case you do have one of these long films you reset the counter after the first 36 frames and continue. If the motor stops almost immediately after resetting then you know that you have tried to reset twice. The system will not allow more then 72 frames to be exposed without reloading.

The counter may be used to limit a shooting sequence. If a series is supposed to be shot of no more than 15 frames, then you set the counter to 15. The motor will stop after the 15th frame, saving you the trouble of having to count. However, you will have to note down the position, deduct the frames exposed and reset the counter.

One thing that you may find confusing is that the counter on the camera counts in an increasing sequence, while the one on the motordrive counts down, otherwise it would not be able to cut-off the shooting sequence at the correct point. The two counter positions therefore never tally. Even so, you should get used to it.

Motor Functions

The functions switch on the motor drive has five

positions apart from OFF, motor function inactivated, normal manual film transport, manual rewind not possible. To reset; depress the unmarked button and turn the knurled button until the white index marker points to the required position.

○ **In Single Frame Position "S"** each press on the release will take just one shot. The release has to be released and depressed again for the next exposure.

○ **In Series Position L** (= Low or slow, lowest position) the camera will expose at 2 frames per second as long as the release is held depressed.

○ **In Series Position M** (= Middle) the camera will expose at a rate of 3 frames per second.

○ **In Series Position H** (High or Fast) the rate is 5 frames per second, provided the motor drive is powered by the rechargeable unit NP-90M. With alkaline batteries in unit BP-90M the rate is 4-4$^{1}/_{2}$ frames per second.

○ **In FP Position** (= Focus Priority) the camera will release only if focusing is satisfactory.

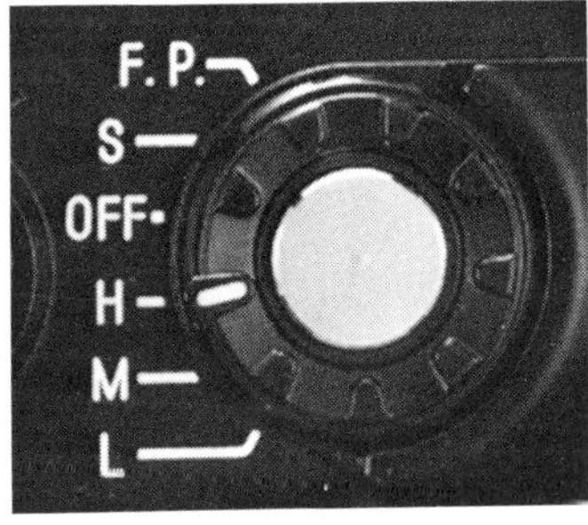

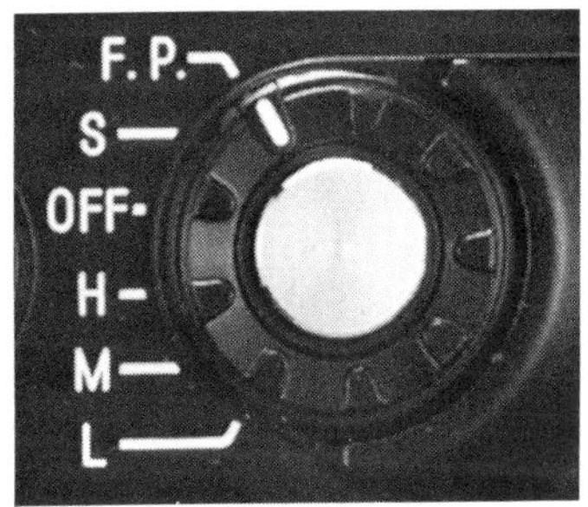

Motor Drive MD-90:
Functions Switch
FP = Focusing priority
S = Single frame mode
H = High rate serial shooting
M = Medium rate serial shooting
L = Low rate serial shooting.

A condition for all these serial functions is that the shutter speed is sufficiently short – at most $1/250$ second for position H and at most $1/60$ second for positions M and L. The motor operates only after the shutter has completed its sequence and longer shutter speed will decrease the shooting rate as a consequence.

There are several ways to release. Generally one releases by depressing the release button. The usual auxiliary functions are activated, i.e. exposure metering, continuing automatic focusing and focusing lock. Holding the camera in the horizontal format is the most convenient position.

The energy units have an additional release on their right hand side, which is sometimes more convenient to use in upright format. The left hand supports the camera and operates, if appropriate, the focal length ring of an attached zoom lens, the right hand activating the motor release that is now located on the top right of the combined unit. The release has to be slightly depressed to activate the metering circuit as it has no sensor switch. The focusing process starts only after the switch has been slightly depressed and the focusing setting is stored immediately, it will not follow the subject. To refocus the finger has to be lifted from the release, which must then be pressed again.

To prevent inadvertent release in normal camera position, the slide switch next to the motor release is pushed down to uncover the red dot and at the same time covering the white dot. This will lock the motor release. This switch is inactivated if the camera is switched off, but may be used when the motor is off (functions switch to OFF, manual film transport). The motor release's only function is to close the release contact via its connection to the camera, it is otherwise unconnected to the motor, apart from being positioned inside this unit.

Finally it is possible to release via remote control cable

or other remote release arrangements (see "Remote Control").

Film Rewind

The display lamp at the left lower side at the back of the motor unit will light up green after each exposure. The same lamp will light up red as soon as the counter switches the motor off, a sign that the film should be rewound. If the frame counter is set for a larger number than available on that particular film, then the film itself will stop the motor. In this case the lamp will light up red. If this is the case, start rewinding without previously stopping the motor. If the motor is switched off and then switched on again for rewinding it will initially pull at the film and may tear the perforations.

To rewind, push the counter reset key in the direction of the arrow and at .the same time depress the rewind key to the left of it. The film will now rewind quite quickly (6-7 seconds for 36 exposures), stopping just before the end of the film is completely rewound into the cassette (this can be done manually, if required).

Apart from the last few centimetres, the film cannot be rewound manually if the motor is attached because the rewind release button is only accessible via the rewind key on the motor. Should you have to rewind manually, perhaps because the batteries are low, then you will have to remove the MD-90 first, then the release button at the bottom of the camera may be depressed and the film rewound as described in the chapter "Camera and Film".

Multiple Exposures

The multiple exposure key (see "Multiple Exposures" in the chapter "Principles of Exposure") which allows several exposures on one frame by preventing transport to the next frame, functions also with motordrive. This is particularly useful for sequences of movement studies. Such shots should be taken in front of a dark background to show the partial images sufficiently differentiated against the dark background. Particularly effective images may be produced by using a synchronized flash with the motorized shooting series; see "Flash Photography with Motor Drive".

Operation is very simple, although the rather small key is not particularly handy. Depress, and keep depressed, the multiple exposure key. Expose a pre-determined frame sequence by setting the number of frames on the motor counter, release the key and depress it again. The last exposure will be an unwanted shot that has to be taken to transport the film. Therefore it is necessary to allow for this extra shot when setting the number of frames. The last unwanted frame can be avoided if you release the multiple exposure key just before the last frame whilst still keeping the release depressed. The timing of this is rather difficult and it is usually safer to sacrifice this one extra frame at the end of the series.

The frame counter on the camera remains at the same position, while that of the motor drive will count on. The latter therefore has to be reset after taking a series of multiple shots. You have to deduct the number of frames shown on the camera from the total number and reset the motor counter.

Motor and AF

One additional autofocus function is possible in conjunction with the motor drive, that is Focus Priority. This means that the release is locked until the subject within the target rectangle is in sharp focus. This avoids repeated out of focus sequences.

For this shooting mode you select FP (focus priority) on the functions selector on the motor unit, point at the subject, depress the release and follow the subject in the viewfinder. The shot will be taken as soon as the green signal appears in the viewfinder and the bleep tone is heard, if this is switched on.

Using this shooting mode requires a little practice. The motor will keep running and exposing more frames as long as the subject is kept in sharp focus (up to 4 frames per second). Therefore you have to be prepared to let go of the release quickly. On the other hand it could happen that the focusing mechanism is unable to catch up with a fast moving subject and so you don't get a single shot. In the latter case perhaps a manual presetting to a point that the subject is approaching may help. The Minolta 9000 can take the shot as soon as the subject runs into sharp focus. For very fast objects though this is no guarantee of success, because the subject could move from the moment the focusing setting is stored and when the shutter is released. It is therefore advisable to use this FP mode for subjects that are not moving too rapidly with respect to the camera.

If you wish to do without the constant adjustment of the focus setting then you can take the sequence in either the L, M or H serial modes. In these modes the camera will be sharply focused in the first frame and maintain this setting for the whole series without re-adjusting the focus, i.e. until you have let go of the release.

Flash Photography with Motor Drive

For shooting sequences with motor drive the flashing rate has to correspond to the shooting rate. Using the

Program Flash 4000 AF powered by the rechargeable battery set, and with flash set to MD you are able to shoot flash illuminated sequences of 2 frames per second. The same applies also to Program Flash 2800 AF in LO-output setting. In the latter case it is important to keep on monitoring the exposure check signal to ensure that the illumination is sufficient, because the flash output is rather weak.

Using control grip CG-1000 and the rechargeable battery pack the frame sequence is even faster because the recharging rate is increased. Using the same flash output settings it is now possible to achieve up to 5 frames per second; i.e. motor in H-function.

Remote Control

With motor drive, remote control is exceedingly useful. The remote release is of only limited use without the motor drive, because you have to return to the camera after every shot to transport the film to the next frame.

On the Minolta 9000 the release is electric (the release button closes electric contacts) and the remote release is therefore particularly simple. The contacts for the release circuit are accessible from the front via the remote release connector. All that is required is a switch that closes the contacts which release the exposure and transport the film on to the next frame.

There are several switching possibilities for the Minolta 9000. The simplest is by remote release cable RS-1000. This 50cm long cable carries at one end a three-pole plug which fits into the remote release connector on the camera, and on the other end it has a hand switch. You have to ensure that the groove on the plug is in the correct position. The RD-1000L remote cable is similar to the above, except that it is 5m long and therefore often more useful.

186

Depressing the switch when the plug is connected and the camera switched on will release the shooting sequence, including motorised film transport. A slight touch on the hand release will activate the exposure metering and autofocus metering with focusing lock; when the release is fully depressed the exposure will be made.

The button on the hand release may also be secured (depress and move in direction of arrow until a red marker appears). This is useful for long exposures, manual shutter speeds position B, and for shooting sequences with motor function set to H, L or M. In the time exposure mode the shutter will open when the hand switch is depressed and stays open while it is kept in the locked position, until it is released again. In shooting sequences, the camera will continue until the film is used up or the counter has counted down to zero.

Remote control is not always safe. The subject on which the camera is supposed to focus may not always remain within the focusing target field of the Minolta 9000. If this is likely then it may be best to focus the camera, either manually or by AF facility, and then select M for manual focusing on the AF switch. It will be necessary anyway to use a fixed focusing distance if a remotely controlled shooting sequence is supposed to cover a subject at a certain distance.

On the other hand it may be possible to work in focusing priority, setting to FP on the motordrive, when shooting moving subjects eg. animals in their natural habitat. This requires a certain amount of luck. After all, the camera can only assess whether the subject within the target field is in sharp focus and not if this is the subject that you wish to take.

Continuous focusing is not possible with remote control; this is due to the fact that the remote release switch does not possess a sensor switch. When the hand switch is lightly touched, the lens will focus on the subject within the target field and this setting is then stored. The focusing setting is retained, even if the subject moves out of the set range. Refocusing will take place only after the finger has been raised from the release and it has been touched again.

Infra-red Remote Control IR-1N

This instrument set allows wireless remote control, however only with manual or preset focusing. The range is 60m, no cables or other connections between camera and photographer are necessary.

The remote control consists of a receiver and a sender. A 9V battery (size 6F22, 006 P or Mn1604 or the appropriate rechargable types) power the receiver. Two batteries, size AA, power the sender. The little lamp on top of the receiver should light up when depressing the battery test button (B.C.) after loading the batteries.

The receiver is either inserted into the accessory shoe of the camera or by means of the supplied bracket, particularly if a flashgun is to be used.
The latter is fixed via the tripod screw at the bottom of the motor drive. Turn the bracket and the receiver so that the receiver cell, marked by a red ring, points in the direction of the sender.

To release remotely (with camera to ON) set the sender to ON (the little lamp at the rear lights up) and the channel selector to the same channel as the receiver (1, 2 or 3). Then point the sender in the direction of the receiver and depress release. The receiver closes its release contact and triggers the release on the camera, at the same time a signal and control lamp lights up above the receiver cell.

For shooting sequences the receiver switch has to be set to C and the functions switch on the motordrive to either L, M, H or FP. The automatic focusing facility is disabled in the remote release mode and the FP position corresponds to the H-shooting rate. The shooting sequence will start on first depression of the release button and will stop when the button is depressed again, unless the film runs out or the motor frame counter stops the sequence first.

If the receiver switch is set to S, then each depression on the release, even continuous depression, will expose one frame, even if the motor drive itself has been set to H or one of the other speeds. In motor drive position S and receiver to C the effect is similar, but the receiver is set to permanent standby. The standby state requires power, but it will release the motordrive set to S only once.

It is only necessary to point the sender accurately, using the orange line of sight on the sender over large distances; at short range it will suffice to point the sender more or less in the direction of the receiver. The signal from the sender is provided by an integrated infra-red flash, just about visible when looking directly at the sender. No permits are necessary to use this equipment unlike the radio release. The channel switch selects various flash impulses. One sender is therefore capable of controlling up to three receivers completely independent from each other. As each receiver closes one contact only, this system can only be used for the remote release; focusing has to be set on the camera itself.

Program Back 90

These days it is possible to obtain databacks for many SLR cameras which allow the date, time and other data to be exposed onto the frame. The Program Back 90 for the Minolta 9000 does all this and offers other timing functions as well.

The program back replaces the normal camera back. Open the camera as for loading a film, push the bolt at the hinge downwards and unhook the camera back. Now hook the program back into the lower hinge end, push hinge bolt downwards and allow the upper hinge end to engage.

The electronic circuit in the program back is fed by two button cells – either silver oxide (SR 44, G13, EPX-76 etc.) or alkaline batteries (LR44, G13A, A-76 etc.). Don't mix the type of batteries. The batteries are located behind a black cover, to the right of the film pressure plate at the interior of the back panel. To remove, unscrew the screw in the cover with a small Phillips screwdriver and insert batteries with positive pole pointing upward.

If the batteries are correctly loaded, a display appears in the rectangular data field at the centre of the back panel, and a dot pulsing at the rate of once a second in the top right corner of the LCD field. This dot always remains visible. If the batteries are run down then the whole display blinks. To check the functions, close the back panel without loading a film, and press the PRINT key at the right of the window: the word PRINT should appear at the left of the black dot. Release, and the PRINT display should blink rapidly 2-3 times. If this does not happen, open the back panel and check that the contacts are clean.

Data Exposure Functions

The date and time has to be programmed the first time the program back is used. These will be retained until the batteries are changed. This is done via the small unmarked input key immediately beneath the data field and the three somewhat larger keys marked MODE, SELECT and INTERVAL.

Date. Depress the MODE key several times until a date appears in the data field (initially 1 1 '80) with MONTH beneath one of the numbers. Depressing the SELECT key will switch the sequence between Day/Month/Year (the usual notation in Europe) or Month/Day/Year (USA) and Year/Month/Day (Japan). To set the date, depress the input key under MONTH until the required number appears (1 to 12), the year ('80 to '79) and day (1 to 31) are selected in similar fashion by their appropriate input keys. According to Minolta the calendar is programmed for the century starting with 1980 to 2079, allowing for different lengths of the months and leap years. In case any of my readers wishes to use the calender after that period, it will continue keeping the time even after the year 2080 but it will have to be reprogrammed after the 1st March 2100 to allow for that leap year.

Time. Depress the MODE key (perhaps repeatedly) until the date and time appear in the form 26 8:22 in the LCD field. Enter the hour via the key in the middle (0 − 23) and the minutes via the key on the right (0 − 59). To set the time to exactly the correct second, set the minute display to one minute less the required time and wait, with exact watch with seconds display in hand, until the next minute has expired and depress minute key again. The date, if not set already, is set as described above.

Frame Counter. Depress the MODE key until three number pairs (or horizontal bars) appear in the LCD field and at the top a plus or a minus sign. The number pairs may be reset from 00 − 99 or to a blank (position between 99 − 00) by depressing the input key. The display will rapidly move through the sequence if the key is kept depressed. The display will count every exposure in ascending order (with plus sign visible) and in descending order when the minus sign is shown. The

SELECT key selects the two signs alternately. The frame counter is disabled if, instead of the last pair of numbers, the bars or the blank are displayed in the data field. If the centre field displays bars or a blank, then only the last pair (00 to 99) will keep count, the pair on the right will remain unchanged. The frame counter will count from one film to the next, it disregards the film leader when a new film is loaded.

Permanent Codes. Depress the MODE key until a six digit number display and underneath it FIXNO appear. The number display will remain the same from one frame to the next. This code is set similarly to the frame counter, if required also with horizontal bars and blanks. Date, time and frame counter continue their functions, whether displayed or not.

Data Exposure. If PRINT is displayed in the LCD field, then the displayed data is being exposed on film. Which of the possible displays should be exposed onto the negative may be selected by depressing the MODE key (possibly also the SELECT key). Exposure is by tiny LEDs in the right lower corner of the frame. The film speed setting in the Minolta automatically controls the intensity of the LEDs. Exposure of this information should be as much as possible to make it visible on the photograph.

Timer Functions

One of the displays after depressing the MODE key (repeatedly if necessary) is INT.S. This may be used to control up to four timer functions. The required function is selected by depressing the SELECT key, displaying INT.S, INT.I, INT.F and INT.L, by numbers, in turn. The timer function refers to shooting sequences but these work only if the motor drive, set to S-function, is attached to the Minolta 9000.

Start Time. INT.S determines the starting time (date, hour, minute) at which an exposure, or a series of exposures, should commence. The time is entered via the input keys in similar manner to entering the actual time and date.

Interval. INT.I determines the time interval between exposures. This may be programmed up to 99 59 59 (99 hours, 59 minutes, 59 seconds). Entry again is via the input keys. The interval has to be larger than the shutter speed plus duration of film transport.

Number of Frames. INT.F determines the number of frames to be taken (the right number pair between 1 and 99). If the interval is long enough it is possible to change the film if required. The series will stop if the last frame on the film is exposed.

Long Exposures INT.L controls long exposure times, provided the camera is set in manual operation to BULB. The exposure time can be set to a value up to 99 59 59, similar to INT.I function. This is not really feasible as the batteries would be exhausted before that because the shutter consumes power in the BULB position. If the camera is not set to BULB then INT.L should be set to 00 00 00.

Interval Release. For time-controlled functions the camera should be securely placed (e.g. to record a laboratory experiment). As soon as everything is set up, depress the INTERVAL key. This starts the shooting sequence, and the first exposure will be made at the point programmed in INT.S. Should you wish to release immediately, then the point of time entered via the right input key is set to --; the exposure will be made one second after the INTERVAL key is depressed. If a system flash is connected to the camera (e.g. the Program Flash 4000 AF) in timer function, then the flashgun will automatically be switched on one minute before the exposure and turned off 15 minutes afterwards, provided the intervals are longer than 15 minutes. The flashgun should be connected to the mains, via mains adapter, for very long exposure sequences.

The exposure data and timer functions may be combined. It is therefore possible to shoot in timer function and to expose the data onto the negative. Select the required data via the MODE key; above the data field the display INT (= interval function active) will appear. Autofocus does not work in timer function; the camera has to be focused when the scene is set up. Depressing the INTERVAL key will interrupt a sequence in progress.

Program Back Super 90

This more sophisticated version offers all the above exposure data and timer functions in a slightly different form. The data is exposed onto the negative in a 10mm long and 0.6mm wide strip on the righthand side of the frame. With this model it is also possible to expose the shutter speed and aperture at which the exposure was taken. The back of the. panel displays exposure data curves on a LCD panel for various shutter speed/aperture combinations for the different program modes (aperture priority, shutter speed priority, etc.) Furthermore it is possible to program exposure sequences with different shutter speed/aperture combinations at preset intervals (from $^1/_4$ to 2 EV intervals). A memory function calculates average values from up to eight individual metered values or selects the

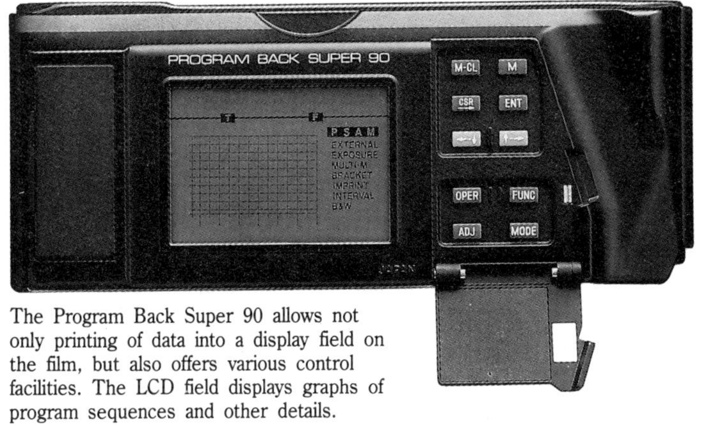

The Program Back Super 90 allows not only printing of data into a display field on the film, but also offers various control facilities. The LCD field displays graphs of program sequences and other details.

longest or the shortest metered exposure as shadow or light value.

Large Film Magazine EB-90

The 36-exposure cassettes are rather limiting for motorised shooting, and particularly so for remote controlled shooting. The large film magazine increases the capacity to 100 frames. The magazine is loaded with film in special cassettes. It is also possible to reload the film bought by the metre and Minolta supply a special film loader FL-90 for this purpose. The EB-90 is used instead of the normal camera back and this has an auxiliary motor for film transport. Contacts on the MD-90 form the connection to the power supply in the EB-90. A viewfinder eyepiece extension is also integrated with the film magazine as it covers the one on the camera. This eyepiece also has eyesight corrections from +1 to −3 dioptres.

The facilities of the Program Back Super 90 are particularly attractive with the 100 exposure magazine. The EB-90 therefore has all the functions for use with the Super 90.

Summary of Data Displays

The variety of metering and operating facilities offered by the Minolta 9000 has to be used in connection with the information conveyed by LC displays. Once the camera is regularly used the observation, operation and use of these displays will become almost second nature. The following summary should help to familiarise the user at the start. On the left is an example of the type of display: the circular display represents the LCD field on top of the camera; rectangle within double circle, and the rectangular field below is the information shown in the viewfinder. The double circle represents the shooting mode selector; if this is omitted then the display applies to all shooting modes. The arrows indicate flashing displays. If applicable, the LED flash symbol is shown, but not the LED for AF mode.

Display	Description	Explanation
	All displays empty	Main switch is OFF, or no battery in camera.
	Only cross bar in LCD field	Main switch is ON, metering not activated
	Shutter speed display but no aperture	No lens attached to camera, applies to all shooting modes

196

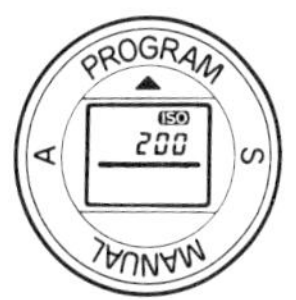

Film speed value with "ISO" in LCD field

Last set film speed, after loading film and releasing to advance leader; appears also when depressing ISO key.

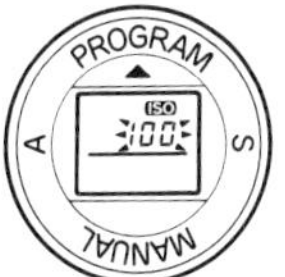

Film speed value flashes

Battery container re-inserted after having been removed, film speed has not been reset.

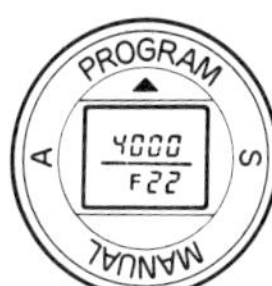

Fastest shutter speed smallest aperture, no shooting mode in viewfinder

Automatic setting when advancing film leader to advance to first frame.

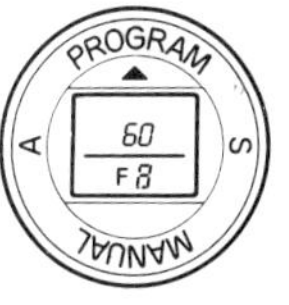

Shutter speed and aperture value, P in the viewfinder

Aperture and shutter speed value selected by program mode

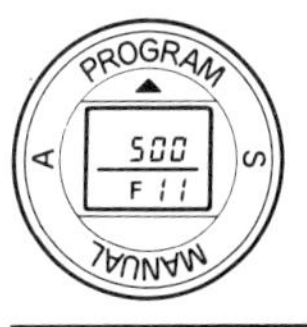

As above, P flashes in the viewfinder

Program mode with shutter speed or aperture value correction by user (program shift)

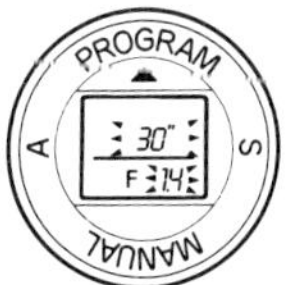

Aperture value and Shutter speed flash, the P in the viewfinder is not flashing

The slowest available shutter speed and aperture value: lower setting limits are exceeded, camera unable to select a longer time and a larger aperture; similar when shortest time and smallest aperture are exceeded

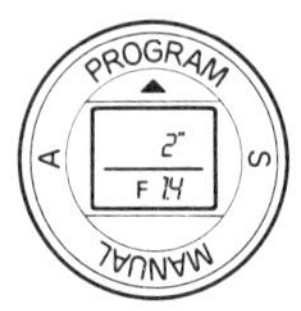

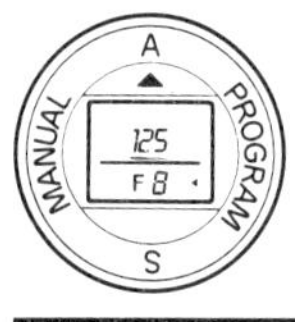

Metering type display flashes in viewfinder in all shooting modes

Lowest metering limit: light insufficient for metering range. Danger of under exposure, appears usually with above display. Similar to upper metering limit with very short shutter speed and small aperture.

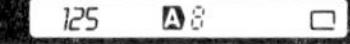

Shutter speed, aperture with arrow point (A in viewfinder)

Aperture priority with aperture preselection

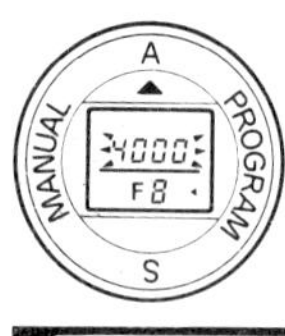

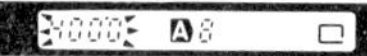

As above, time flashes also in viewfinder

Shutter speed setting limit: danger of under exposure for the preselected aperture. In very poor light the longest available shutter speed of 30 seconds may flash

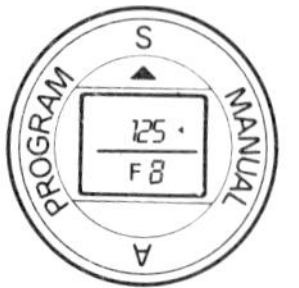

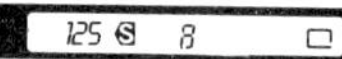

Aperture, shutter speed with arrow S in viewfinder

Shutter speed priority with shutter speed preselection

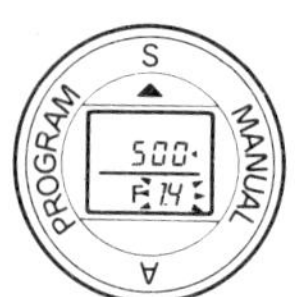

As above, aperture flashes also in viewfinder

Aperture setting limit: danger of under exposure at the preselected shutter speed. For very bright subjects and long time the smallest aperture (22) may blink

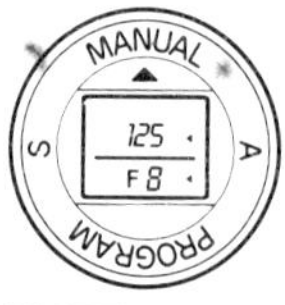

Arrows pointing to aperture and shutter speed in data field, in the viewfinder also M and +0

Manual operation: display of selected shutter speed and aperture. The +0 indicates that the selected combination will produce correct exposure.

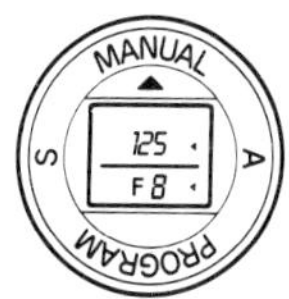

As above but viewfinder display with −2

Manual operation: −2 means that the selected setting will result in an underexposure of two stops (EV−2). (If this factor is chosen as greater than 6½ stops, then −6½ or +6½ will blink)

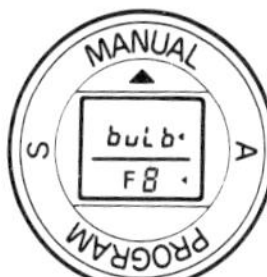

Display "bulb" in the data field and viewfinder, no exposure correction value

Long exposure setting in manual operation

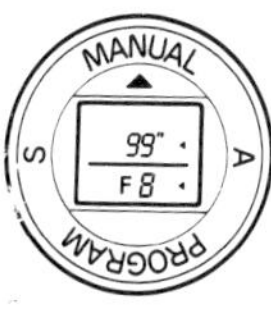

Shutter speed display during long exposure

Shutter remains open until pressure taken off release button, display counts time in seconds until 99 sec, then starts again at 0 secs.

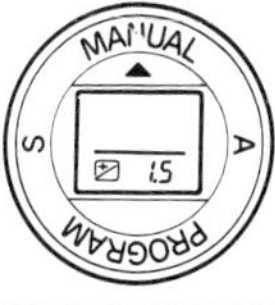

Only the exposure correction visible in viewfinder and data field (in all shooting modes)

The exposure correction value is set by depressing the +/− key and operating the shutter speed key

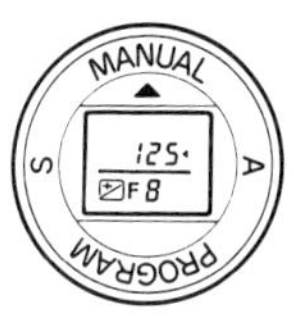

Correction value or indication appears in addition to exposure value

As soon as +/− key is released the exposure display returns, the correction value remains

AF System lenses for the Minolta 9000

Focal Length	Lens speed	Angle of View Hor.	Diag.	Smallest Aperture	Elements/ Groups	Closest focusing distance (m)	Max. repro ratio 1:	Dimensions (mm or g) L	D	F	W
Fixed focal lengths											
24 mm	2,8	73°	84°	22	8/8	0,25	6,3	44	65,5	55	215
28 mm	2,8	65°	74°	22	5/5	0,3	7,7	42,5	65,5	49	200
50 mm	1,4	39°	47°	22	7/6	0,45	6,7	38,5	65,5	49	235
50 mm	1,7	39°	47°	22	6/5	0,45	6,7	38,5	65,5	49	185
50 mm Macro	2,8	39°	47°	32	7/6	0,2	1,0	59,5	68,5	55	310
135 mm	2,8	15°	18°	32	7/5	1,0	6,3	83	65,5	55	365
300 mm Apo	2,8	6¾°	8°	32	11/9	2,5	7,1	238,5	128	42*	2480
600 mm Apo	4	3½°	4°	32	9/8	6,0	9,1	449	169	42*	5300
Zoom lenses											
28–85 mm	3,5–4,5	65–24°	75–29°	22–27	13/10	0,25**	4,0**	85,5	68,5	55	490
28–135 mm	4–4,5	65–15°	75–18°	22–27	16/13	0,25**	4,0**	109	75	72	750
35–70 mm	4	54–29°	63–34°	22	6/6	0,32**	4,0**	52	68	49	255
35–105 mm	3,5–4,5	54–19°	63–23°	22–27	14/12	0,41**	4,0**	87	68,5	55	495
70–210 mm	4	29–10°	34–12°	32	12/9	1,1	3,9	152	72,5	55	695
75–300 mm	4,5–5,6	27–6¾°	32–8°	32–38	13/11	1,5	3,9	163,5	72,5	55	850
100–200 mm	4,5	20–10°	24–12½°	22	8/7	1,9	9,0	94,5	69,5	49	375

* slide-in filter in barrel
** in macro range
L–length
D–diameter
F–filter diameter (usually screw-in filter)
W–weight